Max   ʳallah and
was ᵇᵒʳⁿ   ᵉll-known
illustrator and humorist, and a mainstay contributor of
comic verse to the Peculiar Poetry anthologies. His book
ᵃᵇᵒᵘt downshifting in Orkney caused unintentional con-
rsy when it was published.

By the same author

Chucking It All
Bad Girls

the
last burrah sahibs

max scratchmann

Steve Savage
LONDON AND EDINBURGH

Steve Savage Publishers Ltd
The Old Truman Brewery
91 Brick Lane
LONDON
E1 6QL

www.savagepublishers.com

First published in Great Britain by Steve Savage Publishers Ltd 2012
Copyright © Max Scratchmann 2012

ISBN: 978-1-904246-38-1

Typeset by Steve Savage Publishers
Printed and bound by SRP Ltd, Exeter

contents

PROLOGUE

dawn of the bush era

Our story begins on a hot August night in a packed-out cinema in Hamburg in 1970. The picture palace in question is showing Robert Altman's then brand-new *M*A*S*H*, in English, and has drawn a huge crowd of specky young Germans, together with a liberal smattering of backpacking foreign students.

You find me as a gawky fourteen-year-old erupting with acne, sandwiched uncomfortably between my mother and my father, two stocky Brits from Dundee in Scotland who are frequently mistaken for expelled kulaks from Stalinist Russia, and, of course, it goes without saying that none of us have ever heard of the afore-mentioned enfant terrible, Altman, or even his rising stars, Donald Sutherland and Elliott Gould.

Stopover lowbrow tourists in the bustling Jutland city, and with not so much as a word of German between us, we have nevertheless had a fun day out, having successfully navigated the busy town centre using only our imperial arrogance; stormed an in-store restaurant and ordered a meal by getting a war-veteran cook hauled from his kitchen to wait at our table; and, this evening, by sign language alone, persuaded a long-suffering taxi driver to take us to a cinema with an English-language film on the bill.

Suffice to say that we have completely no clue who we have come to see or what *M*A*S*H* will be about.

Dyed-in-the-wool old-school colonialists, my parents and I have just spent the last three years in splendid isolation, living the forgotten life of the old British Raj in what is now called Bangladesh, then East Pakistan, where cinema has consisted of whatever mixed bag of English-language films the distributors have been able to lay hands on, usually of a print quality that is something short of appalling. Mixed-up or missing reels, unspeakable dubbing, and, of course, draconian censorship have become the norm to us, and the sexual revolution of nineteen-sixties indie directors has not so much passed us by as never quite reached us.

Nevertheless we settle amicably in our seats as the lights go down and adverts for Coca-Cola and Kleenex with dubbed-on Teutonic jingles run their course, then, with an unaccustomedly seamless reel change, a short art-house film starts up which is to be the defining watershed of my young life.

A swaying handheld camera zooms in on a young girl walking through a suitably Bavarian forest, with odd jump cuts to strangely phallic pine cones and toadstools, while the girl's voice is overdubbed onto the soundtrack, treating us all to an endless monologue of which I understand not a word. But the film is obviously comic since the German audience are all beginning to chuckle, and my family appear to be the only spectators who are not getting the joke.

However, the girl has stripped down to a purple and mustard bikini by now, and is lolling provocatively against a tree when a male voice speaks, and, without any hint of coyness, she reaches for the fastener on her top as though she intends to remove it.

This, of course, piques my interest considerably, although, after three years of Islamic censorship, I don't expect to be witness to any major revelations, and, though every boy in my school had sat with bated breath watching Sophia Loren shuck down to her undies in *Yesterday, Today and Tomorrow*, we always knew that the camera would turn tastefully away before the last garment hit the floor.

However, this time the customary jump cut to another scene does not happen, and the catch is unfastened and the top slides off, and I think the audience are still laughing, but it is hard to tell over the roar of blood in my ears.

But the girl's endless monologue is continuing unabated, as she – oh my god – slips her pants down in full view of the camera's unimpeded gaze, while the oblivious audience just keeps on laughing, unaware that they have just been provided with the answer to the question that has haunted the restless and fevered dreams of an entire generation of prepubescent males.

Yes, life is unquestionably the closest that it has ever come to being perfect on this hot summer night, and my definitive erotic experience is only marred by the fact I am sitting in a cinema with my father on my left-hand side, and my mother on my right...

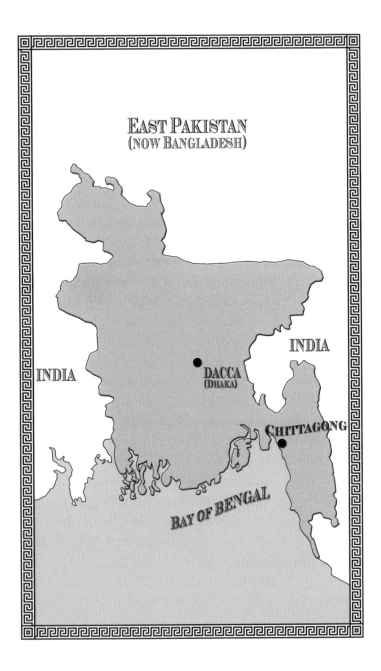

EAST PAKISTAN
(NOW BANGLADESH)

INDIA

INDIA

● DACCA
(DHAKA)

CHITTAGONG ●

BAY OF BENGAL

CHAPTER 1

1967 - boeing boeing

Three years earlier, to the day, sees us in Karachi airport at four in the morning. We have just stepped off a ten-hour flight from London, with only a couple of stopovers in hot dusty transit lounges in the war-torn middle east, and we are, unsurprisingly, completely exhausted and worn out.

The Karachi transit room, however, is cool and sparse, and devoid of the myriad of fast-food franchises that would characterise a modern air terminus, but there is air conditioning and comfortable seating, and we flop down gratefully to wait for the final leg of our flight to be announced. Yet, even in our semi-comatose state, it seems that something is not quite right, and as the dust settles, we realise that there are only about ten weary travellers in the quiet room, and that the various airline desks which line the opposite wall are dark and deserted.

My dad anxiously scans the departure board but it is blank, and other travellers who have staggered up behind him begin to voice his silent fear that there might not be a connecting flight tonight.

All eyes quickly turn to the only manned airline desk, and the PIA clerk behind it gulps nervously as he clears his throat.

ॐॐॐॐॐॐॐॐॐॐॐॐॐॐॐॐ

'Gentlemen and their good ladies, please, good evening,' he stammers in a quaint, but well-spoken voice. 'Gentlemen and ladies wishing to continue their journeys to Dacca and Chittagong, please be advised that your PIA flight will leave promptly at nine o'clock this morning, whereupon a delicious English breakfast will be being served. Please take rest now and wait patiently. A very good night to you!'

On the last syllable he snaps off the light on his green illuminated sign and makes a bolt for the safety of the staff-only door at the rear of the hall, but a fellow traveller, who had earlier introduced himself to us as Dr Khan, moves in like a quarterback in an American movie and intercepts him neatly.

'Just one moment,' he says, his good-looking face stern, 'what are you saying, you fellow? There is no flight till morning?'

'Uncle,' the squirming clerk stammers, 'it is four in the morning, there is no one flying aeroplanes at this hour...'

Dr Khan treats him to his best you-have-a-terminal-disease-and-I-don't-care glare and shakes his head disgustedly, still barring the unfortunate's way as he addresses my dad.

'My friend, I have been in UK for four years slaving at the Birmingham Royal Infirmary, and today I return to my homeland. Yet this is the welcoming committee that they send. You, fellow, get us a taxi, we will go to a hotel!'

In the background some Iranian students who have boarded the flight at Tehran are laying claim to the couches and fashioning their hand luggage into makeshift pillows. If I wasn't too young to know what the word meant, I would have said it was an omen.

'Uncle,' the hapless clerk wheedles in a Uriah Heep-like gesture of supplication, 'we cannot get you a hotel. You have not yet been through customs.'

'So, we will go through customs, I have nothing to hide.'

'It is four o'clock in the morning, Uncle, there are no customs officers on duty. In the morning your flight will be ready and PIA will serve you a fine breakfast. Go and take rest now.'

'This is preposterous...' the good doctor begins, climbing deftly onto his high horse, as my dad quickly steers my mother and myself to three vacant sofas. 'There'll be no flight tonight,' he says quietly.

When the departing British partitioned India in 1947, some bright spark designated the two main Islamic areas, separated by a thousand miles of hostile Hindu territory, as the new state of Pakistan, and thus we find ourselves stuck in an airport lounge on the wrong side of the great divide waiting for a 'local' flight in the middle of the night.

Still, the transit room is calm and cool, and the couch feels good to my tired bones. 'Dad, have we been to Karachi before?' I ask sleepily as my father makes a pillow for me from my school blazer and covers me with his jacket.

'Once, when you were little, when the steamer stopped at the docks and we went on a trip here. But you won't remember...'

Dimly, in the back recesses of my mind, I can see the interior of a black and yellow taxi and hot streets with rickshaws and camels. 'There were camels, and it was hot,' I murmur, 'really, really hot. And it was really smelly...'

'Yes, that's right, Chummo,' Dad says patting my shoulder. 'But it's nice and cool in here, so you try and sleep for a bit, there's a long day ahead tomorrow.'

'OK,' I smile to him, just as there's a loud clunk from the ventilation shafts and the air-conditioning dies. A soft muttered 'Ufffgh!' rises briefly from the nomadic camp that's just sprung up, and then silence again, as the temperature slowly begins to rise.

'And I've really met Wallace?' I mutter, as my heavy eyelids grow heavier.

'Yes, but you won't remember him, you were only two or three,' Dad reassures, but I have already crossed over to the other side, and I dream of camels and hot streets, and Wallace, who looks like a demented Santa Claus in colonial fatigues, letting a deranged monkey out of a box, and all the king's horses and all the king's men can't ever make it cool again.

I wake to the sound of bustle and tinny voices announcing flights. The airline desks, so like a ghost town the night before, are now peopled by smiling women in strange hats, and new travellers with hand-luggage mill around the now lit-up departures board.

The Khan family breeze in, having dragged some hapless official out of bed in the middle of the night to pass them as fit to go to a hotel. The doctor, his neat moustache still razor sharp, looks slightly more dishevelled than the previous night, but his wife is resplendent in a fresh sari, and sails into the busy room like a brightly-painted ship's figurehead.

'My friends, my friends,' the good doctor says effusively, 'you should have stayed with us. I argued with that fellow until half past six in the morning. This is not the UK, you know, you have to tell these fellows what to do or they will do nothing.'

My dad nods, knowing well the mentality of bureaucrats in the subcontinent, but the doctor has already charged forward, beckoning us to follow. 'Come. Come. We will all get on the plane, these fellows have kept us waiting long enough, you there, peon, make way!'

The Khan party surges forward and we quickly follow. The air conditioning has been restored inside, so the early morning heat hits us like a white light as we step out onto the already steaming tarmac, our waiting plane a gleaming silver bird against a cloudless blue desert sky.

Pretty girls in green outfits greet us as we board, handing us each a scented wet towel as though it were the crown jewels and chirping, 'PIA welcomes you aboard your flight,' to each of us in turn.

Another girl seats Dr Khan and his wife at the front of the cabin and my mum and dad at the opposite side of the aisle. She smiles genuinely at myself and Dr Khan's son, Iqbal, and ushers us into the seat behind. 'So, I am putting you two naughty boys together, and, after breakfast, if you are good as gold, I will allow you to come and visit the cockpit,' she offers as a bribe for good behaviour, before departing with a friendly wink.

Iqbal looks over at me, dishevelled and somehow incongruous in this heat with my blazer and British school uniform. 'You been here before, man?' he asks in a thick Brummy accent.

'Yes, no,' I say, hesitatingly, 'just India, I was born in India...'

'And you're going to Dacca?'

'Chittagong.'

'Chittagong? You're going to Chittagong? That's the end of the world, man. Fight for day school. They'll try to board you out when they see the schools there!'

At Dacca we say goodbye to the Khans and leave the comfortable jet to shuffle across the now burning tarmac to an old Fokker Friendship, which sits, its twin propellers idling, ready for take off. These sturdy little planes have been in service since the fifties, and this one looks like the prototype model, its bodywork pitted from frequent storms and its green PIA livery peeling and parched. There is no roped-off area to the boarding ladder, but the pilot, who is standing smoking by the landing gear, beckons us forward, and a single girl in a sari welcomes us aboard, this time sans the aromatic cool towels of the Karachi flight.

The little planes only hold about thirty folk on a good day, and this one is already packed to the gunnels, but we manage to squeeze aboard and Dad bags me a window seat as we taxi past the corrugated-iron hangars and out onto the main runway and then, with surprising agility, up into the air.

Ascending from Karachi we had flown over a parched desert landscape, but the countryside around Dacca is lush and green, and we are soon over rice fields and large stretches of water, passing perilously close to little island villages where naked children cheer and wave at the big silver bird in the sky. Soon the flourishing alluvial plain gives way to azure blue water as we cut across the magnificent Bay of Bengal, and then swoop down to Chittagong, a bustling port town on the coast, with miles of sandy beaches and acres and acres of agricultural land leading inland towards its verdant green hills.

My dad leans over me and looks out of the tiny porthole as the runway rushes up to meet us, 'We're here now, Chummo,' he murmurs with a trace of anxiety in his voice. 'I hope they've sent someone to meet us.'

'Probably a damn rickshaw,' my mother complains, getting into her stride. 'I told you to get a definite time from them, you can't trust these bally people...'

'It'll be fine,' my dad reassures, exuding a confidence he doesn't feel as we all scan the tiny brick terminal building. 'Wallace will have set something up for us.'

'Oh, you and your damn friend Wallace,' Mum rejoins, as we struggle down the rickety wheeled staircase to the tarmac in heat that feels like the backwash off a blast furnace. 'We'll be lucky if we get something better than an open truck. Max, don't slouch, and fix your tie, they might have sent someone important!'

'Who?' I ask, looking at this place that is easily five hundred miles past the end of the world. 'Who could possibly know us out here?'

As if in answer there's a loud shout from the open doorway of the tiny terminal and a stocky man with close-cropped ginger hair, and dressed in the customary jute wallah's whites, rushes out and grips my flabbergasted father in a fierce bear hug.

'Chic, you old bastard, you've finally come. I knew when I wrote you couldn't resist the call of the soil for ever. Retire us? Those bastards in government house can't retire us till we're good and ready to go. And who's this bastard? This can't be Max, can it? Why, the bugger's as big as a Rangoon rickshaw wallah. Come and give your Uncle Wallace a hug, boy!'

I'm engulfed into arms like the jaws of a steel bear trap and I catch the fleetingly familiar scents of jute dust and sweat, and, before I'm summarily dropped onto the ground so that Wallace can whirl my little round mother into the air, I get a momentary flashback of a previous and happy life, and, suddenly, I know that, despite all its strangeness, we have come home.

Films about the Raj always depict the British in India as tight-lipped Englishmen sitting stoically in their tuxedos in the heat of sweltering tropical nights, and whereas these kind of people did exist, they weren't our people.

My dad and his ilk were the Calcutta Jute Wallahs, a ragtag bunch of lowbrow Scots, mainly from the grey Presbyterian metropolis of Dundee, who had manned the myriad of mills along the Hooghly river for generations and were now grasping at the last years of the old colonial lifestyle in the hot and dusty machine shops of East Pakistan.

Thus, when we enter the tiny little air terminal building at this forgotten outpost, there is a huge cry of welcome as a myriad of weather-beaten Scotsmen embrace my parents and slap me heartily on the back.

However, Wallace, a long-time buddy of my dad, and the person who has been instrumental in luring us out here, propels me past the crowd and through an outer tier of shyly smiling native under-managers and their bejewelled wives, and leads me to a gaggle of kids who are seated on top of two wooden benches, swinging their bare feet over the seating area.

Most of them are young indigenous lasses in brightly coloured clothes, but in the middle, and obviously holding court over their entourage, are two dumpling-faced white girls about twelve years old, dressed in print frocks and little white socks and sandals.

'So, Max, do you remember my twins, Harriet and Elsa? You used to roll around naked with them when you were nippers,' Wallace laughs by way of introduction. 'Harriet peed on your leg once, didn't half make you howl!'

The aforementioned Harriet makes a face. 'Don't you mind Pop, boy, we're going to be great friends. We've got you a fine gun and we'll show you how to shoot next week, if you're game?'

I nod, still in a world where guns are plastic James Bond replica pistols from British toyshops, when the second twin claps me gruffly on the back and says, 'Yes, I brought down three damn moonya birds by the river this morning, patach, patach, patach! I'm one hell of a crack shot to beat, so you'd better be on your form, boy. Come on, let's go wait in the car...'

I'm about to dragged out into the inferno that is the car park when my mother's voice cuts through the maelstrom with a howl of anguished rage: 'They've lost our luggage? What do you mean, they've lost our luggage!'

It seems that, after managing to follow us successfully from Dundee to Dacca, our luggage has not made the last leg of the journey, and it is decided that my mother and I and most of the entourage should head 'home' while my dad and Wallace remain at the airport to collect our baggage from the next flight.

I'm herded into an old Austin with the twins and two little girls who don't appear to speak any English; an old Dundonian called Barry ('He's still living with the Indian woman, you know,' I hear Peggy, Wallace's wife, whisper to my mother as I'm bundled into his car); and a tall fair-skinned West Pakistani called The Captain, who is something very important in the mill my father has come out to manage.

Next to Barry's Austin stands a dark blue Vauxhall Victor, which is to be ours for the duration of our stay.

A tubby driver with a cheeky grin loiters in the meagre shade of the airport building, but he hastily stubs out his cigarette and lumbers over to open the door as my mother and Peggy approach, followed by a flotilla of bashful under-managers' wives in their best saris, all hot cerises and peacock blues, gold embroidery flashing in the baking afternoon sun.

Everyone else is being bundled into a ratty old Volkswagen minibus, but, before the dust has had time to settle, the Vauxhall speeds off in a cloud of dirt, and I realise that I am eleven years old and alone in a car full of maniacs in a very foreign land. However, I've no time to feel insecure as Barry takes off after the speeding sedan, his horn blaring as we cut out into the main thoroughfare, a bumpy, dusty road jam-packed with cars, bullock carts, cycle rickshaws and gaudily painted trucks.

'Faster, Uncle, faster!' the twins cry, hanging out of the windows without fear of imminent decapitation by the honking lorries. 'Let's race that fellow and teach him a lesson!'

Barry grins and accelerates, swerving past wavering baby taxis, the twins swearing loudly in Bengali at their drivers, but the car ahead spots his ploy and leaps forward into the afternoon traffic. On the right-hand side of the road there are busy docks and breakers' yards with towering ships at anchor, and on the left sun-baked jute godowns and small bamboo kutcha houses and shops, which soon give way to jerry-built concrete structures as we get nearer to the town.

The noise is deafening and the three o'clock sun is white-hot and punishing, bouncing off the tarmac in shimmering mirages that blind stoic white bullocks as they pull their heavy loads towards the factories and markets of the city. Inappropriately dressed in a blazer, nylon shirt, school tie and heavy synthetic grey shorts, I feel like I'm being broiled alive in the hot tin can that masquerades as Barry's car, and I silently take my handkerchief from my pocket and wipe the sweat off my face as the twins continue to hang out of the open windows and exchange insults with street urchins who sit on top of high whitewashed walls.

'You hot, man?' Harriet, the slightly more human of the two enquires. 'Take that jacket off and get some breeze.'

'Yeah, what you in all those clothes for?' Elsa chimes in, appraising me with her practised slaughter-man's eye. 'You look like an office baboo who's forgotten his umbrella!'

The twins find this analogy hilarious and translate it into Bengali for the benefit of their friends, who giggle disproportionately, and Barry, catching my despairing eye in the rear view mirror, winks and says, 'Aye, you're no in Dundee now, Burrah Sahib!'

After about thirty minutes of interminable traffic we head out of the bustling town again, and the houses and shops thin and give way to acres of rice fields stretching out across the flat river plain to the sea. The road climbs up onto a man-made embankment, taking it about four or five feet above the level of the patchwork of wet fields and potential flooding, and the clear surface acts as a red rag to the driver of the Vauxhall, who makes the jump into hyperspace and shoots ahead, disappearing into a little blue dot on the distant horizon.

'This fellow thinks he's Stirling Moss,' Barry mutters as he struggles to keep pace with the car ahead, but the twins look at him blankly until the quiet captain explains: 'An English racing driver.'

Eventually, as the traffic begins to thicken again, high barbed-wire-topped walls whitewashed in the customary jute mill turmeric yellow appear on the left side of the road, while kutcha houses and small shops suddenly crowd onto the right. Women pause in their labours in front of their small huts, and tiny children shout and point at the car-loads of white people that now perambulate through their quiet village.

'Bloody gundas!' Elsa mutters disgustedly, but further comment is lost as the car rounds a bend and we find ourselves enmeshed in the thick of a herd of untended native cattle, strange humpbacked beasts that British farmers would send straight to the glue factory, and our three-car convoy picks its way slowly through their midst, horns blaring.

'Is there much further to go?' I ask the Captain, who seems the safest bet out of the resident inmates, and he smiles kindly, as though seeing this tired and bewildered white boy for the first time.

'Oh no,' he says calmly, 'you are home now,' and, next to a square-shaped pond filled to the brink with limpid green water, I see large British-era cast-iron gates bearing the words 'Victory Jute Products' in an arc of rusty iron letters. The Vauxhall honks its horn aggressively and the gates swing inwards, and we follow inside as a moustachioed Pathan durwan proudly salutes our arrival.

Arriving for the first time at an Indian jute wallah's house
is a bit like showing up for a weekend house party at a
British stately home in the height of the season, and a
line-up of servants by the door is not uncommon. Today,
however, as Barry's car drives under the flaming red
bougainvillea arch to the salute of yet another hairy-faced
durwan, there is no welcoming committee of men in
white livery assembled outside the spacious, if not
palatial, bungalow, and we walk in alone.

The twins rush off to rip brass fittings from the doors
as trophies, and I slink gratefully over to my mother's side
as we walk cautiously under a high stone arch and onto
the cool black and white checked marble-floored veranda
that surrounds the house that is to be our home for the
coming three years.

A short pot-bellied man, bare-footed and dressed in
white cotton trousers and a long white muslin shirt,
strides out of open French doors to greet us, his arms open
in a gesture of welcome and his smile warm and genuine.

'Aunty, Aunty, welcome, welcome, I have waited for so
many days for your safe arrival in our land. I trust that
Manager Sahib will also soon be arriving. These fellows at
the airport are in need of one good slap to wake them up.
Come, come, come inside, we have prepared tea in your
honour.'

He gestures expansively and leads the way inside,
signalling us to follow, and we all pile into a large airy
sitting room with plain whitewashed walls and comfortable, if old, settees and armchairs.

'Sit, please, sit,' the smiling man beseeches, as ceiling fans lazily stir the warm afternoon air round the big room, and we all take our places around a low table spread with wilting European-style cakes and pastries.

'Do you know who he is?' my mother whispers to me, as chipped pre-partition china cups and plates are handed around.

'Maybe the Burrah Bearer,' I reply, taking my best guess, but my mother shakes her head.

'No, he's too well-spoken for a servant,' Mum muses in one of her famous not-too-discreet stage whispers, 'but the damn fellow's dressed like a bally baboo.'

The Captain, who's seated himself to my left and formed a barrier against the twins who are busy demolishing the cake salvers, intervenes diplomatically, and speaks directly to my mother, saying, 'This is Zahidee Sahib, Aunty, he has been our beloved manager here these three years past, but is now leaving us to work for his cousins in West Pakistan.'

My dad and Wallace eventually show up at about five, thankfully bearing suitcases, and there is much speculation on just how much abuse Wallace has had to heap on the heads of the airport officials in order to achieve this miracle. More and more tea is served, and the assembled multitudes show no sign of leaving, until, at seven o'clock sharp, Wallace rises up from his seat, claps his hands authoritatively and announces that it is time everyone went home.

Jet-lagged and exhausted as I am, I still want to jump up and kiss his florid cheeks with gratitude, but content myself with coming to the veranda doorway to make sure that all the crazy people actually vacate the premises completely. I've lost my blazer somewhere along the way and have had to abandon my shoes after inadvertently standing on an ant-hill courtesy of the twins, but I still look and feel like an extra from an Ealing boarding school comedy who's wandered inadvertently onto a Bollywood film set.

Mum has already vanished inside the house, and Dad puts a friendly arm around my shoulder as the last car vanishes under the blazing bougainvillea, and he leads me inwards, saying, 'Well, this is probably the only time in your life that you'll be willing to go to bed at seven.'

We stroll tiredly back into the now quiet house together, and thanking the smiling cook who offers a supper of yet more tea and sweet biscuits, Dad takes me through to the room designated to be my bedroom, where I flop gratefully onto the bed.

And then cry out in disbelief.

The bed is a plain, wooden divan, with a lumpy unsprung horsehair mattress, and landing on it feels like flopping down onto a bed of hard-compacted earth. My dad plumps it with his hand and mutters, 'We'll get you a new one tomorrow, Chummo. Come on, you can sleep in our room for tonight,' but any further plans of rest are quickly interrupted by the sound of loud hammering and my mother yelling, 'Chic, Chic! Where are you? I'm locked in the bally bedroom. The damn door's gone and jammed!'

CHAPTER 2

baᴣaar biᴣarre

When I wake the next day the sun is already bright and clean, the morning air fresh and scented from the summer flowers outside. My father has, inconceivably after the previous night's shenanigans, gone off to the mill at six a.m. to mark his new territory, much to the shock and awe of his fleet of under-managers, and Mum has monopolised their en suite bathroom, so I pad down the long marble-floored hall to the other bedroom to use the facilities there.

This shady room is bigger than my bedroom back in Dundee, cool and echoy, and there is, thankfully, an English toilet, plus an ancient recycled porcelain sink and a huge built-in marble bath with a large chromed shower hanging precariously over it. I fiddle with the taps and, predictably, there's no hot water, but the day is already warm enough not to need it and I stand gratefully under the steady stream of cool brownish liquid, inhaling the forgotten aromas of anti-prickly-heat soap and medicated shampoo.

Abandoning my British school uniform I dress in clean summer shorts and a striped Marks & Spencer's tee-shirt, little knowing that I'll be able to sell it on the black market when I outgrow it in a few months' time, and wander through to a comfortable dining room furnished with an old teak-wood table and sideboard.

My mother is already ensconced at the head of the table like the resident dowager and, as there's apparently no bearer as yet, the cook from the previous night waits patiently by the table.

'What eat, Chotta Sahib?' he asks me in English, and fighting back the urge to ask for Coco Pops, I remember my years of Indian training and reply, 'What you will bring me, Botchi.'

The cook grins at my correct etiquette and vanishes off through a gloomy pantry where a huge 1950s American fridge hums contentedly, and we soon hear him banging pots in his kitchen beyond.

My mother, the duchess, who looks like the last four years in Scotland have been surgically expunged, pours herself more tea and informs me that we will be going to the market this morning, as soon as 'some damn baboo' arrives from the mill with money for her to equip the house with 'decent crockery and sheets'.

'Is anyone else coming?' I ask cautiously as the cook piles about a week's supply of eggs and toast and a jar of guava jam in front of me, beaming, 'Eat it all now, Chotta Sahib, grow big and strong,' but when my mother says it will be just us, I readily agree to join the expedition.

The cook and my mother now enter into a long and involved conversation about menus and something called meatless days, so when I finish my eggs and toast I wander out to the pillared veranda to investigate the grounds properly.

Our flat-roofed bungalow, which seems to have been built in the late fifties, is large and roomy but nothing like the mansion-houses we have previously occupied in India. It sits in a sizeable garden with a lawn about the size of a small football field to the front, with a vegetable patch, bulky chicken coop and a coppice of banana and guava trees to the rear. There's an eight-foot-high wall all around the gated property, and bougainvillea and other climbers have been planted to conceal the barbed wire and broken glass that tops it, but I can nevertheless make out the minaret of the local mosque and the thatched rooftops of kutcha houses that have been built onto the other side of our fortifications.

All is pretty much as I've expected, except that at the far back corner of the vegetable patch, screened from the house by a thick jungle creeper festooned with luscious red flowers, there's a mysteriously empty corrugated-iron shed that smells like the circus, and when I return to the dining room I ask the cook about it.

'Ah, Zahidee Sahib,' he tells me sadly, 'he kept a cow, and we made fine butter and ghee. Those happy days are over now.'

'Gosh, Mum,' I say, eyes bright with possibility, 'I'd love to keep a cow. Can we…'

'No way,' my mother interrupts, slipping back into a vocabulary that proves that we have, indeed, spent the last four years in Dundee. 'Not a chance in hell.'

The aforementioned 'damn baboo' eventually shows up with the requisite rupees, and we pile into the dark Vauxhall, which, on close inspection, bears many dents and scratches from near misses with bullock carts and lorries. The driver who had so frustrated Barry the previous day opens the back door for my mother but signals for to me to join him in the front seat. He's a mischievous-looking man in his mid thirties, with inky-black skin, thick curly hair and the customary pencil moustache, and I immediately sense an ally.

'What's our driver's name, Mum?' I ask in English.

'Ask him yourself,' my mother replies. 'Speak in Hindi, it's almost the same as Urdu, he'll understand you perfectly.'

I frown, summoning up words that have lain dormant for almost a third of my young life.

'Tumhara naam kya hai?' I stammer hesitatingly, and a huge smile spreads across the driver's dusky face.

'You speak Urdu, Chotta Sahib,' he grins, 'I will not be able to have any secrets in your company. Do you also speak Bangla?'

'No, only Manager Sahib speaks Bengali,' I reply, finding the forgotten words flowing back, and the driver nods knowingly.

'So, Chotta Sahib,' he says expansively, 'my name is Mafzal, and I live in the village beyond the gates. I have a wife and eleven children and my own paddy field and a very fine cow.'

'Don't even bally well ask...' my mother threatens in English.

We virtually fly along the elevated road through the patchwork of rice fields, small wet squares of green paddy encased in low mud walls, where women and small boys heft heavy copper pans of water from the irrigation ditches to their fragile crops. It is August and the end of the rainy season, so the water is plentiful, and an ornate waxy-leafed plant, christened water hyacinth by the British, grows copiously over all the wet surfaces, its pale purple flowers resplendent in the bright morning sun.

Mafzal speeds along the highway, skilfully avoiding stray cows, goats and cyclists, but eventually is forced to slow down as we near the outskirts of the town and stalled traffic tails back into our path.

The Vauxhall eventually comes to rest in a small bazaar, a mixture of kutcha and brick-built shops, and stops parallel to a small boxlike establishment bearing the weathered English signboard, 'Shokutt and Partners – Fine Art Dealers'. The front of the store is open and unglazed, and on its three inner walls hang row upon row of gaudily hand-coloured pictures, much in the style of Pierre et Gilles, of Muhammad Ali Jinnah, the Virgin Mary and some monkey-faced Italian pin-up girls in bikinis.

I've been so intent on this dazzling display of colour that I haven't noticed the rest of my surroundings, and suddenly become aware that in the two or three minutes we have been at rest a small crowd of children and casual bystanders have gathered, and they stand quietly peering into our car like peaceable zombies from a PG-rated version of *Night of the Living Dead*.

'What are they all staring at, Mum?' I ask, not wholly comfortable.

'Oh, just us,' my mother replies matter-of-factly, 'all these bally gundas do it, you'll soon get used to it again.'

The traffic ahead starts to move and Mafzal slips the car into gear and we surge forward along a badly pot-holed road, but we have only gone another few hundred yards when we come to a stop again at a closed railway crossing gate.

'The people of Chittagong wanted a bridge over this railway and raised the money for it by public subscription,' Mafzal explains to us, 'but the contractor was a chorr wallah and his concrete was bad, so we still have to always be waiting by this gate.'

'Is a gate so bad?' my mother asks diplomatically but Mafzal shakes his head in the way of one who knows better.

'Ah, Memsahib,' he says gloomily, 'the gates are shut according to the train timetables, and often the trains are many hours late...'

We eventually hit the centre of town, which is a wide dual carriageway called Station Road. There's a huge cemetery on a hill to the left, which abruptly gives way to rows of street-front shops, while a bustling fruit market heaving with overflowing baskets of late season mangoes sits noisily on the right-hand side.

The two horn-blaring lanes of traffic are divided by a thin strip of raised grass where there have once been trees and ornamental flower beds, but these have now been colonised by street dwellers and strange Heath-Robinsonlike structures made from bamboo and flattened-out ghee tins are affixed to the old colonial railings.

Women sit by cooking fires stirring things in copper pots as Mafzal elbows the car into a tight parking space on the main thoroughfare, blasting his horn and hurling abuse at a bullock cart driver attempting to unload his cargo, and a mob of half-naked urchins surges forth from the shanties and immediately surrounds us, hands outstretched, crying, 'Hello, baksheesh, Aunty!' in shrill strident voices.

Mother gets out of the car like visiting royalty, brushing the kids aside with a brisk 'Jaao! Jaoo!' but we have barely cleared them when our way is barred by a cripple on a strange wheeled contraption like a low-slung skateboard. The man's eyes are limpid pools of misery as he looks up at me like a Hallmark puppy dog, his withered legs hanging useless beside him on his grubby cart.

'Please, Chotta Sahib…' he beseeches, and I immediately reach for my pocket and the single rupee note I have been given earlier.

The beggar's eyes light up as he identifies an easy mark, but Mafzal's hand shoots out and intercepts mine, whispering, 'No, no, Chotta Sahib,' and my mother turns to me witheringly, snapping, 'Do you remember nothing of India?'

'But the poor man's crippled!' I protest as I'm dragged away. 'Someone has to help him!'

Mafzal and my mother exchange a look. 'His parents bound his legs when he was child, so that he could beg,' Mum explains patiently, and Mafzal adds, 'It is permissible to give him some coins on a Friday or holy day, but never ever a note, or we will all be robbed blind!'

After four years in Dundee, where shops consist of the somewhat presbyterian local Co-op and a trip to Marks 'n' Sparks on a Saturday afternoon, the bustling centre of Chittagong is a fantasia of outlandish colours and scents. The wide boulevard-style pavements built by the long-departed British seethe with open-fronted stalls, most comprising just a dais for goods and their cross-legged proprietors and then a rush-mat roof to fend off the blinding afternoon sun.

While the fruit sellers tend to congregate exclusively on the right-hand side of the road, there is no real rhyme or reason to retailers on the left, and a toy stall selling cricket bats and gaudily-coloured plastic balls happily rubs shoulders with a grain merchant's, while at the end of the row there's a wizened old man with a henna-dyed beard offering black magic aids, and bits of offal in jars of alcohol sit cheerfully amidst dried crocodile feet and an assortment of animal teeth.

'Come, Memsahib, these street-front fellows are all thieves,' Mafzal says, beckoning us towards a maze of narrow alleys, and we follow him into a netherworld of stalls and open-fronted brick-built shops, offering everything from brightly-coloured plastic shoes to exotic-looking dried fruits and groceries. The combined smell of spice and animals and dirt here is overpowering, and even my mother, raised in the east, has to give in and reach for a cologne-soaked handkerchief from her red plastic handbag as we proceed deeper into the seething labyrinth.

A pedlar carrying a bamboo frame laden with papier mâché masks calls to me to purchase from his wares, while small boys with strings of firecrackers round their necks vie with him for my trade, darting in front of fat bearded men who try to push squawking chickens into my face. Bhangra music blares stridently from crackly Tannoys outside music stores, and, as we round a bend, we come face to face with the local meat market, a collection of low daises spread with coarsely butchered carcases, heads and offal sitting cheek by jowl with prime cuts, and everything crawling with slow-buzzing flies.

I can feel my breakfast starting to rise up, and Mafzal, spotting my discomfort, suggests that maybe the new market might be a better bet for the Chotta Sahib on his first trip to town.

The 'new market' in question is a two-storeyed concrete mall boasting long aromatically-scented tunnels of cool shade and hundreds of merchants selling everything from imported sweets and groceries to tinny Japanese transistor radios. Mafzal, spying a paan vendor outside, tells us to wander as we choose, and we perambulate down a long parade of fabric shops, all pleasantly incense-scented and stocked to the roofs with bright cotton prints, rich velvets and silks in all the hues of the rainbow.

Crockery vendors call out to us in English as we emerge into their quarter, and pot-bellied men in singlets and lunghis beseech us to inspect their mishmash of wares. My mother brushes their overtures aside with an experienced eye, however, tutting disdainfully at the glowing displays of enamelled cups and coarsely-painted delft plates, and, when we finally grace a large fancy goods emporium with our presence, the proprietor himself puts down his bubbling hookah and emerges from his den at the rear, calling for chairs and bottles of ice-cold 7-Up to be brought in our honour.

Dinner service after dinner service is paraded for our benefit, some in trendy sixties patterns, others somewhat more antique in their design, and, although I am greatly enamoured of a tea set commemorating the coronation of Queen Elizabeth, we eventually settle on a Heal's-style blue and white striped ensemble. Junior assistants arrive with tea chests and straw to wrap everything, there being no original packaging anywhere in sight, and my mother and the shopkeeper lock in mortal combat to negotiate a price, which, after various accusations of daylight robbery and protestations of certain bankruptcy, is finally reached, and our purchases are loaded into the back of the waiting car.

CHAPTER 3

heat and rust

The next day slips by relatively uneventfully, the quiet pace of our new lives being interrupted only by the arrival of workmen bringing furnishings from 'storage' to the sparsely fitted house. Carved chairs with coats of arms from the British East India Company have appeared in the dining room, and lowering colonialist wardrobes with spotty mirrors and heavy teak-wood doors are installed in the bedrooms, a discreet carpenter arriving to fit a hefty brass padlock to the 'money shelf' in my mother's personal armoire.

Our prim, slightly fidgety cook, who is, ironically, a Buddhist and therefore a strict vegetarian in his personal diet, knows the full British-Indian repertoire by heart and forgotten dishes like Pish-Pash, Glacé Beef and Potato Chops appear on the table in strict rota each night. There is still the matter of employing a bearer to be dealt with, however, as the cook is having to buy and prepare the food and serve it at table and then wash up after. News travelling fast, on the morning of our fourth day a bearded old man dressed in a prayer cap, lunghi and long muslin shirt comes to the house with a young boy not much older than myself to fill the position.

The next day is Friday, the Muslim Sabbath, and we have been invited to spend the sunlight hours with Wallace's family, this marathon involving my mother and myself arriving in time for lunch with Peggy and the twins, and then my father following on after work in time for afternoon tea, culminating in the two families sitting down to dinner together at seven. It sounds like hell on earth to me, but my mother is keen that I create a good impression and I keep my seditious opinions to myself.

The new bearer, who will soon be nicknamed Alfie, is already being bullied unmercifully by the cook, but has been permitted to bring toast to the breakfast table for the first time, under his superior's eagle eye, of course, and I quietly point to the correct spot on the starched white cloth to save him from further rebuke when he gets back to the kitchen.

'We will be at Wallace Sahib's house all day today,' Mum tells the cook, 'so only the Manager Sahib will want lunch, then you can have the day to yourself.'

'Very good, Memsahib,' the cook replies in English just to frustrate Alfie who flashes me a beseeching look of long suffering. 'I am hoping that you will have a jolly time.'

'Oh, I'm sure we will,' Mum mutters under her breath.

Just as we are getting ready to leave for Camp Wallace, a plaintive melody echoes out across the gardens and through the house, and I realise that it is the song of the muezzin in the mosque over the wall calling the faithful to prayer. Used to India and – quieter – Hindu temples, my mother rolls her eyes heavenwards in true British fashion in the face of this new eccentricity of the east that must be stoically borne, but I secretly feel that this haunting mantra is one of the most beautiful sounds that I have ever heard.

Mafzal, who has little time for religion, is irreverently chewing paan when we go out, but he grins a cheerful greeting as we pile into the car and promises to have us at our destination in double-quick time, taking off like a bat out of hell and almost knocking over the bearded durwan who hurries from his prayers to open the gates.

Victory Jute Mill is, astoundingly, not on a river, but Persistence Works, the factory which Wallace runs with a fist of iron, sits in a traditional waterside location on the banks of the swirling Karnaphuli, and Mafzal soon has us flying along a verdant canal road lined with banana trees and lush vegetation.

I'd expected a mansion-house, but Wallace's abode is another modest colonial bungalow, a good bit older than ours and painted in the warm turmeric yellow so beloved of mill architecture. It sits with its back to the quiet factory road, its pillared front veranda facing the turbulent river, and the open kitchen windows greet visitors with wafts of heat and spicy aromas.

Two squawking chickens lie on the ground with their feet bound as we walk up the drive, but before I have a chance to ask my mother about their purpose the twins – the same pair of little girls that had been at the airport – thunder out of the house and descend on us both crying, 'Aunty, Aunty, why have you waited so long to come and see us!'

Peggy appears in the open doorway and ushers us inside to a darkly-furnished colonial living room with animal skins on the floor and framed pictures of rifle-toting white men in raj topis on every available surface. The room has French doors all along the river side, which in turn lead to a shady veranda, where comfortable cane furniture is arranged in a semi-circle looking out towards the water.

As I am to discover is the norm for Chez Wallace, an entourage is assembled, and the twins are seated on the veranda steps, while perched primly on the edge of one of the cane chairs like a hunched mynah bird sits a small nunlike Anglo-Indian woman in a plain black frock.

'This is my friend Mary Magdolina, Max,' Peggy introduces, 'she helps me look after Harriet and Elsa.'

'Do you say your rosary night and day, Max?' the skinny woman asks earnestly, gripping my hand in her snarelike fist and fixing me with a beady-eyed stare that makes Madhur Jaffrey in *Cotton Mary* look well-balanced. 'Aunty, do you make sure that he says his prayers every day so that his immortal soul will not perish in the flaming fires of hell?'

'I go to Sunday School,' I manage to squeak, but the little hunched woman mistakes my discomfort for flippancy.

'God will punish you for that, you wicked boy,' she whispers in my ear with no trace of humour in her voice, 'even when you are dead and lying in the cold of the grave, God will come to you and say, "Why did you neglect your prayers, you bad, bad boy?"'

'Girls, why don't you show Max around the garden,' my mother quickly interjects before the Nun of Monza can have me crucified to set an example, and the twins obligingly wrench me down the steps to the lush lawn uttering war whoops of delight.

'She's such a help,' I hear Peggy saying to my mother as I pass out of earshot.

The rest of the morning passes agonizingly slowly, much of the time being spent watching the twins killing small birds with their point-two-two rifles, but lunch proves to be an unexpected high point in an otherwise tortuous two hours. My dad, like many other colonials of his generation, does not permit Indian food to be served at his table, and our diet, so far, has consisted solely of the rather stodgy British-Indian fare that I mentioned earlier. Wallace, however, is a true son of the soil and has no such culinary hang-ups, and we sit down to a magnificent lunch of aromatic curried chicken served with heaped salvers of saffron-coloured pilau rice studded with almonds and little flecks of silver leaf.

The closest I have come to curry since I left India at the age of six has been of the Pickering's tinned variety, a particularly odious nineteen-sixties British concoction of turmeric, cornflour and unaccountable quantities of raisins, and so this delicious repast, which is concluded with heaped bowls of chilled watermelon, to my young eyes more than makes up for doing without any number of the imported luxury goods that Chittagong lacks.

Wallace is in fine form and regales us all with anecdote after anecdote during the meal, even making the tightly wound Mary Magdolina almost laugh on occasion, and an almost deathly silence descends when he retires to his bedroom for his afternoon siesta. The one o'clock sun is white-hot and punishing, and even the twins pause in their blood sports and vanish to their rooms to take a bath, while my mother and Peggy settle down quietly to play cards together on the veranda.

The entourage have departed for home and their own beds, and there is something blissfully soporific about sitting on the cool marble floor of the veranda in the shade, listening to the sound of the breeze in the trees and the swish of the fast-flowing river, interrupted only by the gentle noises of cards being laid on the old baize table.

Half an hour passes delightfully, and I am just about to allow myself to think that life cannot get any more perfect, when the bottom falls out of my world as I overhear Peggy say, 'Of course, you'll have to put him into school soon. There's an excellent military academy about a hundred and fifty miles along the road from you where he can board during the week. They'll have him shooting properly in a couple of months and make a proper sahib out of him!'

'Chic's not keen on boarding schools,' I thankfully hear my mother reply, 'is there any place local that's good?'

'Well, the twins go to the convent school, but they won't take a boy his age,' Peggy muses. 'But you could always try the brothers at Saint Peter's...'

CHAPTER 4

the small print

Scarcely a week has passed, but we have already adjusted to the local clock and are going to bed at nine and rising around six. The rains are almost over, and, as we approach September, the early morning temperatures start to move towards pleasant, and my mother unveils her plan for next year's crops in the market-garden-sized vegetable patch at the rear of the house.

The garden already supplies the household with cut flowers, potatoes, bananas and pineapples on a regular basis, as well as guavas, papayas and sugar cane when in season, but my mother, inhabited with the spirit of Gertrude Jekyll, proposes to add rotating hardy crops of sweet corn and tomatoes in the main growing area, with more delicate cauliflowers, aubergines and peas to the rear as the fierce sun and rain will allow.

Completely infected by the gardening bug, we go off to visit the fragrant nursery in the city to buy seeds and bedding plants, and, much to my father's amusement, several young mango saplings to add to our already ample fruit grove.

The malis are busy planting these now, and, not wishing to be excluded from the fun, my mother and I wade out barefoot in the wet and fragrant earth to help, burying the tender roots in the loamy soil and never doubting the word of the soft-spoken man at the nursery who has

assured us that we will definitely see fruit within two years.

My life has never felt more like a perpetual holiday, and it's not until I'm washing my feet down at the standpipe that I notice the small, slightly nervy man in a neat white shirt and Oxford bags who stands patiently on the back veranda.

'Hello, who are you?' I ask in Urdu, and he beams a crocodile smile at me, replying in English, 'I am Mr Hussain, the tailor, Chotta Sahib, your dear Amah has called me to measure you for your new school clothes.'

Nothing quite prepares me for the sight of my new school, and I stand at the edge of the huge concrete playground quite dwarfed by its sheer magnitude.

I have just spent the last four years learning the ins and outs of life in a Scottish inner-city primary, which, although it seemed like Sodom and Gomorrah to begin with, pales into insignificance when compared to the pile that now stands before me.

St Peter's High School has grown exponentially from its humble beginnings as a mission school run by a handful of hardy Benedictine monks in the eighteen-fifties, and the present red-brick L-shaped building stands three storeys tall and boasts around two thousand students. Each floor consists of an endless line of brick arches, which give a few grudging feet of shade to the innumerable classrooms that sit behind, and, even in the noisy street facing the playground, I can hear the sound of fearful boys' voices chanting multiplication tables and irregular verbs.

All the warm feelings of belonging of the last few days drain away as I contemplate what is about to come, but my mother, in an uncharacteristic gesture of warmth, squeezes my hand and whispers, 'It is not always going to be so strange. Now, don't make a damn fuss and we'll go and meet the headmaster.'

On the opposite side of the playground and overlooking a tin-roofed whitewashed church that sits surrounded by coconut palms to help keep it cool, is the school administration block. There is a parents' waiting room at one end; then a busy office with grilled windows where Brother John, a taciturn Canadian, holds sway over the intake of fees; and, finally, in the shadows of the end of the row, sits a small dark room with a saloon-type door that bears the unassuming sign, 'Principal'.

A voice calls 'Enter' to my mother's knock, and in the dim room beneath a huge crucifix where a contorted figure of Christ neatly bleeds onto him, sits a quiet man dressed in a spotless white cassock, who simply says, 'Ah, this must be Max. Leave him here and I'll call his teacher.'

My first schoolmaster in this Orwellian education factory is a young man in his early twenties known to his pupils as Sir Lester, it being the school custom to address male teachers by their first name prefixed with Brother or Sir. He's a dark-skinned, stocky man dressed in the customary cotton slacks and coloured shirt of the locality, but hasn't as yet fallen prey to the ubiquitous pencil moustache, and he smiles encouragingly at me as he leads me from the principal's office to his classroom.

It has started to rain torrentially with the customary suddenness of a late monsoon shower, and we hug the walls of the admin block before making a run for it across the large concrete playground, then, drenched, bolt into the shelter of the school's red-brick arches, catching our breath before we attempt the stairs.

All the classrooms on the lower floors have glazed windows and electricity, and, as we walk past, I can clearly hear the chants of five-year-olds in the Kindergarten rooms going through their alphabets, while in a narrow laboratory next door, boys of eighteen sit scribbling furiously in dog-eared exercise books.

It is like nothing I have ever seen before, and my Dundee primary with its Victorian high-windowed classrooms and stentorian spinster teachers suddenly becomes quaint and charming by comparison. As Sir Lester leads me up flight after flight of concrete stairs to the top floor, I seriously doubt that I will ever survive in this enormous place.

We have finally reached the summit, where the classrooms have chicken-wire in the windows and no electricity, and, therefore, no fans, and Sir pauses outside an open door where, inside, about sixty boys sit on wooden benches at long six-to-a-unit desks. The din is louder than Bedlam, but he leans back against the unplastered brick wall, out of the sight of his charges, and motions me to stand beside him.

'My friend, the boys will all be very curious about you,' he says matter-of-factly, 'and many of them will tease you because you're different. You'll have to learn to live with that, but if any of them are wicked or they tease you too much, you come to me, and I will thrash the culprits senseless. You follow?'

I nod, still not quite up to making a verbal reply to this brusque but kind man, but I feel my heart sink, as, deep from within, I hear the words, 'Here we go again...'

Dad and me on board ship
headed for Dundee, 1963

CHAPTER 5

1963 – the inevitable flashback

Only a scant four years earlier I had stood bewilderedly at midnight in the bitter January of 1963 at the deserted Tay Bridge Station in Dundee. Britain was experiencing one of the most severe winters on record since the Ice Age, and, amidst serious rail disruption, our train from Liverpool had pulled in to the desolate platform several hours late.

We had just journeyed across the breadth of India by train from Calcutta to join the ocean liner *Circassia* at Bombay for the four-week run to Liverpool and then, this morning, had caught a British Rail 'express' to Dundee, which my parents referred to as Home.

Undeterred by the severe weather, the chugging locomotive from Merseyside had cut its way valiantly through endless snowdrifts which rose above the roofs of its cold carriages as we steamed our way northwards, speeding relentlessly through the towering glaciers of frozen snow that made the journey seem like a surreal trip through Superman's ice castle.

My dad had been in his element all day, excitedly dashing to W H Smith's at Lime Street to buy Fry's Turkish Delight bars before boarding, then leaping from the train at Edinburgh Waverley to procure a pristine copy of the *Dundee Evening Telegraph* and hot mutton pies. Mum had been less enthusiastic, eyeing the icy weather

with a lowering countenance, while my sister June, then just seventeen, had been oblivious, happily reading *The Boyfriend* and other teenage magazines for most of the arduous journey.

I was six and a half years old, and although this was not technically the first time that I had been to Britain, it was really the first trip that I could remember. My life previous to this had been lived in both an urban and natural landscape that was vibrant and brightly coloured, with large, sunny houses and lush tropical gardens, and the tiny cold waiting rooms and grey skies that I had seen today were both puzzling and alien to me.

I had been bought a new navy-blue trench coat and navy and white woollen scarf, and my mother wrapped this latter tightly around my neck as we walked gingerly across the abandoned platform in the cold and somnolent railway station. A sulky porter wearing a heavy donkey jacket over his uniform banged our cabin trunks onto a hand trolley, while the guard at the gate looked over our motley group with an appraising eye, then asked my parents if their names were Chic and Rose.

'Aye, weel,' he said slowly, having been answered in the affirmative, 'there was a lass that said she was your Cousin Bunty that waited three hours for you. She's away home the now, but she said to tell you that she was here. So I've tellt you!'

He looked expectantly at my dad at this point, barring our way until a florin was produced, and then insolently touched the tip of his peaked cap, muttering a mocking 'Much obliged!' as we passed through his barrier.

My mother held her tongue for all of ten seconds before considering herself out of earshot, then exploded, 'The damned cheek of that bally fellow, standing there expecting a tip, I wouldn't have given him two bally annas, let alone two whole shillings!'

'Aye, but things are different here,' my dad said patiently, picking me up and carrying me in his arms. 'Come on, Chummo, let's get a taxi and get you home to bed.'

The old Morris taxi pulled up outside a small, dimly-lit late-fifties semi in a grey-harled suburb. Hard-packed snow was banked up along most of the drive with only a narrow path leading up to the entrance, but the kitchen door opened as we alighted, and a tall heavily made-up woman in a turquoise suit and a large beehive hairstyle rushed down the frozen path to greet us, her furry slippers incongruous with the rest of her fashionable outfit.

'Oh hello, hello, you're here at last,' she gushed, hugging everybody. 'I've had the fire lit this last three hours so your house is like a Turkish Bath indoors. Come away ben and don't stand out in the cold like this. June, you're looking like a million dollars. Rose, is that your sari you're wearing? Oh, mighty, no, it's just your scarf. My, and the weather we've been having, I'd have thought you'd have brought some of that sunshine with you. Or does it not work if you've not brought your magic carpet? Ha ha! That's funny, isn't it, if you'd come on your carpet you'd have been here before now. Not that I could stand it in India, I don't think, all those darkies playing pipes to snakes and things, oh no, I'm a Dundee girl through and through. Well, here we are then, like I said, toasty like one of yon Turkish Baths. I've lit the paraffin heater in the big bedroom, but the wee room was fine. You can put the electric heater on before you go to bed. Well, I'm dying to hear all your news but I'll leave you just now, young Max looks just a bit done for. My, but he's grown, hasn't he? They grow up so fast. June, you'll be having your own soon, ha ha ha!'

She breezed out as fast as she'd breezed in, and we all stood shell-shocked in her wake, staring bemusedly at the tiny room lit only by a low-watt ceiling pendant and an ineffectual standard lamp by the dying fire.

'Who was that, Dad?' I asked, my breath clearly visible in the 'Turkish Bath temperature' room, and my father laughed.

'Why, that's Cissy from next door, do you not remember her? Oh, you must have been too small. Come on, Chummo, let's get you to bed, it's past midnight and there'll be all sorts of ghosties wandering about, and you don't want to meet any of them, do you?'

Dad had carried me through to a large storage fridge with two beds in it while delivering this monologue, and he sat me on the nearer of the two as he reached over to turn on a single bar of a small cast-metal two-bar heater.

'Are we really to stay here, Dad?' I asked in a small tired voice, and my father smiled at me.

'Of course we are, Chummo,' he replied. 'This is Home.'

My father's close family were a group of elderly women known collectively as the Aunties, four grim-faced sisters all widowed by the First World War who had learned to function together as a single organism. My grandmother, fifth sibling and black sheep of the assemblage, had, bored with widowhood, long since fled to America in search of lonely expatriate Scotsmen in need of solace, and the Aunties had therefore rallied together to become mother and grandmother to my father and his offspring.

Thus the first Sunday at Home found us summoned to the stuffy front parlour of Aunty Barbara, eldest sister and, therefore, alpha aunt to the rest of the group. The remainder of the coven were, of course, out in full force, and the three other ladies lined Barbara's gothic pre-war sofa in their fox-fur collars like beady-eyed rooks in a Charles Addams cartoon, all vying desperately to win the attention of 'young Chic', their beloved nephew who had done so well for himself overseas, and I quickly became aware that my mother, sister and myself were very definitely second-class attractions in their eyes.

We had been in situ for just fifteen minutes before the conversation drifted from the terrible weather to the good ladies' favourite pastime of trying to win my father's heart and put my mother down in a single sentence. The Aunties' vitriol and casual racism soon got into full flow as their pace quickened and the tempo of their sport accelerated.

'Chic, do you like those scones?' one of the Aunties would lead. 'I baked them for you myself this morning. Rosie, do you ken what scones are, do they have scones in India?'

'Oh, away now, Aggie, of course they'll have scones in India. They'll be needing them to throw at the tigers likely! Rosie, do you see many tigers or it all just zebras and things where you are?'

'Wheesht, Jean, you're talking nonsense, there's no zebras in India, the tigers will have eaten them all. Rosie, do you do much cooking or do the slaves look after all that? I always think that it's important for a wife to make her man's meals herself, don't you think? I wouldn't be too keen on giving any man of mine something that a Black Sambo had touched with his hands. Chic, now you'll have to have one of my fruit squares, I baked them myself just this afternoon!'

If my father was aware of this familial bear-baiting of his wife he never showed it, and he sat there oblivious, eating the countless dainties that were pressed upon him while my mother slouched stony-faced in her chair like a cartoon character slowly turning into a pulsing pressure cooker.

Being a child who was accustomed to speaking my mind I did not take kindly to this state of affairs, and I tried – valiantly – to divert attention and speak to the group several times, but was summarily shushed with a children-should-be-seen-and-not-heard look from the Aunties. My frustration level was mounting to breaking point when I was rescued by the only friendly face in the room.

'Max, come away ben and help me set the table,' my dad's spinster cousin, Bunty, a sprightly lady in her mid-forties, interjected, taking me by the hand. 'And if you're very good I'll take you down to the garden to build a snowman after tea!'

Greatly relieved, I followed Bunty eagerly down a shadowy hall where the décor boasted cabbage-rose wallpaper and stained Lincrusta and, as if on cue, an old wall clock chimed the hour sonorously. Bunty popped briefly into a small kitchenette that smelt of Brussels sprouts and stirred something in a pot, then took me into an old-fashioned dining room that was colder than the grave.

'You used to stay in this room when you were a baby,' Bunty said brightly, laying cutlery on the starched white linen tablecloth. 'Do you remember?'

'No,' I said, shaking my head and trying to stop my teeth from chattering, 'was I all by myself or did my ayah sleep here too?'

Bunty laughed. 'Oh no, lambie, there was no ayah, just you with your mum and dad and June, you all stayed here on your daddy's last leave.'

'Here, we all stayed here, in this one room?'

'Oh yes,' Bunty replied, 'your dad always used to stay here with us when he was on leave until he got too grand and went and bought his own house.'

'Oh,' I replied, thinking that my dad's leave could not end soon enough so that we could all go home.

My previous school in India had sat in a rambling Arts & Crafts house in a leafy suburb of Calcutta. Lush banyan and peepal trees protected a shady garden, and an open veranda floored in blue and white patterned mosaic led through French windows into the main classroom, where brightly-painted wooden desks housed about fifteen small children in a clear and sunny room.

At the far side of the building was the 'big school', where about another dozen or so kids sat at proper desks with ink-wells, but between the two was the great divide, a richly ornate room with antique rugs on the cracked marble floor and a huge carved wooden desk the size of an ocean liner situated all-seeing in the centre.

This was the home of the formidable Miss Martin-George, a tall and angular spinster with short marcel-waved tresses and a general horsy air. Miss George owned and ran her little school, which was considered the best kindergarten that Calcutta had to offer, with a rod of iron, and all her charges were all taught how to sing, dance and talk 'properly' on top of our basic curriculum of reading, writing and 'rithmetic.

Despite its somewhat Dickensian founder, however, it was a wonderful place for a curious and creative child to be educated, and I was soon winning prizes for art and nature study and left my lessons each day hungry for more. So, imagine, then, my sheer incredulity on my first Monday in Dundee when my dad led me by the hand through the carbolic-scented corridors of an old Victorian Scottish primary school with austere prison-grey walls and high frosted-glass windows and told me that this is where I would now be coming each day.

A stooped headmaster took me to a dimly-lit room at the end of a long corridor, a large cavern of a place lined with cast-iron and wood desks riveted to the floor in strict rows. About forty children in identical navy-blue jumpers and navy and purple striped ties sat with their heads bent over books, and on the high varnished-wood window-sill there lived a rather moth-eaten collection of glassy-eyed Victorian taxidermy in scruffy glass domes.

'Ah, Miss Petrie,' the cadaverous old master intoned breathlessly in a cracked voice that came from deep within his failing lungs, 'I have a new pupil for you. This is Max, a small boy who has come from India and will be in need of an introduction to our ways, I'm thinking.'

I looked up fearfully, expecting some awful moustachioed creature in a long frock with a mortar-board on her head and cane under one arm, but instead I saw an attractive young woman in a short powder-blue suit with black velvet lapels, who smiled welcomingly at me and gestured to a seat in the front row.

There was a muffled giggle from the class as I sat, and someone up the back whispered, 'The new boy's in the dimmer's seat already!' and I experienced a terrible feeling that my overall premonition of foreboding was going to be proved irrefutably correct.

With the headmaster departed the pretty Miss Petrie lost her smile and thwacked her wooden pointer on her desk, announcing, 'All right, children, reading. New boy, you can start. Come out and stand on the floor and read to the class. Your Indian school did teach you how to read, didn't they?'

I had already discovered that the overall knowledge quota of the ways of the east amongst the adults of a town that relied almost completely on the Indian subcontinent for its industrial raw materials was almost non-existent; so it was no surprise that the level of ignorance amongst its children was quite frightening, and my first playtime in a Dundee primary school was the closest thing I had encountered to sheer hell on earth in my short six and half years.

'So, are you a real Indian, then?' a pugnacious boy demanded, poking me in the ribs. 'Did you have to fight cowboys before you came here?'

'Yeah, bet he did, and shot all their wives and children with a tomahawk!'

'What, he killed little babies?' a pigtailed little girl with penny-rounder glasses said incredulously. 'Yukkkk! That means he's a murderer!'

'Yeah, Murderer! Murderer!' they all cried. 'Dirty Indian Murderer! Whooop-whooop-whooop!'

The bleak and icy January eventually gave way to a frost-whitened February, which in turn finally yielded to a windswept March, the grey spring skies ultimately producing sleety rain and a thaw. Gradually, the days began to get longer and by Easter the tiny patch of garden at the front of our house brought forth tentative displays of snowdrops and crocuses. Bunty came to visit, bringing armfuls of bright yellow daffodils, and bought me the coveted chocolate egg my mother had dismissed as 'all damn paper', but I was still counting off the days till our return home, and was overjoyed when our last month in Dundee appeared on the Scottie Dog calendar on the kitchen press.

Dad had a cabin trunk airing out on the back green when I came home from school one afternoon in early May, and he was busy with Anchor Line labels and a bottle of glue as I bounded over to him for a hug of welcome.

'Hello, Chummo,' he smiled, 'did you have a good day at the school?'

I had, in fact, had the worst day imaginable, having just been carpeted by Lurch, our cadaverous headmaster, for trying to beat the non-existent brains out of three boys who had said that I lived in a mud hut up a kookaburra tree, but I answered Dad with a non-committal, 'Not bad,' so glad was I to see that our time in this cold, narrow-visioned township was finally coming to an end.

'So, are you getting on all right at the school now, do y'think?' Dad asked a little too casually, abstractly spreading paste onto labels for only one trunk.

'Ye-es...' I answered cautiously, suddenly aware that something was almost certainly up.

'Well. It's just that, well, your Mum and I, we think that it's important for when you're a big boy that you can tell people that you did all your schooling here, rather than back in India, and we've decided that I'll just go back myself this time so that you and Mum can have all the benefits of staying here...'

I wanted to shout out, 'Benefits, what damn benefits?' but I already knew from other British children in India that what was about to happen to me was a very real danger for expatriate children, and I knew that I had to play this very carefully indeed. However, I was barely seven years old and a traitorous tear let me down, as I said simply, 'But I'll be going to the big school when I get back. I'm very nearly seven now...'

I spent the next four weeks alternately pleading, cajoling and tantruming with frustration, but all to no avail, and at the end of May 1963 my dad sailed back to Calcutta alone. It wasn't unique as abandonments of the time went, and I knew even then that my life in a strait-laced Scottish primary school, however draconian, was better than being dumped in some dreadful boarding school in the middle of nowhere, but at the time it really felt as if my mother and I had been unceremoniously forsaken in a foreign land and been left there to fend and forage for ourselves as best we could.

Communication with Dad over the next three years was minimal, and was limited to the number of words that could be squeezed into the slim blue sixpenny air letters that we exchanged twice weekly, and he watched me growing up via the occasional photograph or eight-millimetre film sent to him by sea mail and therefore three or four months out of date when it arrived.

Talking to him on the phone was, likewise, virtually impossible in those days, and therefore our annual all-too-brief three minutes' worth of crackling conversation was reserved for Christmas or times of national emergency only.

Eventually, however, my life in Dundee became less strange and then, finally, normal, but it was always a poor second best when compared to the breadth and sheer vitality of India, and, with the exception of an agonisingly brief six-week summer holiday, I did not see my father again until 1966 when the Indian government compulsorily retired him and sent him dejectedly home. I was overjoyed when Dad returned to Dundee, but he rattled around in his new and more lowly job like a displaced soul, and remained morosely discontent there until that fateful day in 1967 when a letter from Wallace arrived postmarked Chittagong, and we all set off on our last great adventure together...

Me aged ten in Dundee, 1966

CHAPTER 6

the bitter tea of brother pious

School in Pakistan starts promptly at eight in the morning and runs with only a fifteen-minute recess till one in the afternoon, thereby avoiding the worst heat of the day, but the academic week is a punishing Monday to Saturday and heavy loads of homework eat quickly into my evening hours. On the plus side, however, Fridays are called half-days, with lessons ceasing a little before noon to allow the Muslim boys to get to mosque on time, and there are frequent holidays throughout the year to accommodate all the myriad festivals of the Muslim and Catholic religions.

My dad, like most of his fellow mill hounds, sleeps for an hour each afternoon, and I am sitting alone reading in our shady living room on my first after-school Saturday when a strange buzzing sound interrupts the quiet of the high-noon heat. Tracing the insistent noise, I discover a small grey internal telephone next to the house's main black bakelite original and, lifting the receiver, I utter a tentative 'Hello?'

'Hello? Is that Max?' a quiet voice enquires. 'Max, this is the Captain. I was wondering, do you have any plans for tomorrow, man?'

It takes a second to place the Captain as the diplomatic young man who had driven home from the airport with us on that fateful first day, but, recognition quickly dawning, I greet him warmly and reply that my social calendar is, in fact, completely clear for the following day.

'That's good,' he replies laconically. 'I'm going to the pool, I'll pick you up at ten. You got trunks and things, man?'

The busy pool belonging to the Chittagong Club sits in the partial shade of an ancient banyan tree, with the black and white Edwardian mock-Tudor frontage of the club-house looking down from its vantage point on the hill above. To the left and right of the water there are flat areas of closely mown lawn dotted with regular beach umbrellas, and old wicker chairs and tables cluster greedily in the scanty shade that they throw down.

There is a large company of Japanese steel workers drinking locally brewed beer at a table by the door, but the real party seems to be on the other side of the shimmering blue water. A laughing group of young French people at the first table cry 'Bonjour!' to us, but the Captain and I pass them by and walk to the centre umbrellas, where a vociferous mixed bag of locals and grizzled old whites are lounging in the sun, and I know without having to ask that this is the Jute Wallahs' table.

Whispering his drinks order to a passing bearer, the quiet Captain leads me into their midst, and I am clapped on the back and told how much I've grown by an assortment of pot-bellied old mill hounds and their equally rotund good ladies. It's only eleven in the morning, but the heat is already getting uncomfortable, so I extricate myself and nip quickly into the changing room to slip into my trunks before running out and diving into the clear rippling water of the pool.

There is nothing to beat the delicious chill of cool water in subtropical heat, and, savouring the privacy that being in the pool affords, I swim length after length until sheer exhaustion drives me to the ladder and I step gingerly over the hot concrete slabs surrounding the water and flop down on the grass at the Captain's feet.

Someone hands me a Coke, and I look round to see, seated on a psychedelic pink beach towel, a skinny white-haired lady in her late fifties clad in one of the tiniest bikinis known to man.

'Hello, love,' she says with a friendly smile. 'You must be Chic's boy, you won't remember me, will you? I'm Vera, I came to your Christening party.'

I'm about to utter some pat reply when I notice that the lady's nipples are peeping out from the sides of her carelessly fastened top, and, blushing, I look hastily at my feet and stammer something totally incoherent instead.

Vera, oblivious to my discomfort, continues to regale me with happy baby stories, leaning over me and pinching my cheeks as she does so, and I am only rescued from the hell-fires of embarrassment by a portly man in baggy shorts and a screamingly loud bush shirt who emerges from the shade of the sun brolly to shake my hand.

'Welcome to Chittagong, young man,' he says with a wink, fully aware of what's ruffling my composure. 'I am Vera's good friend, Doctor Ahmed, and this is Cindy, my wife.'

'Hiyah, sweetie,' a strong west coast accent simpers as a petite redhead dressed in a peacock-blue Muslim tunic and pantaloons peers tentatively from the shade. 'Gosh, isn't he tanned already? I'd be a mess of freckles in no time if I went about like that.'

'Ooh yes, he'll soon be brown all over with just a little white bum,' Vera teases, treating me to another flash of limpid breast. 'When's your mummy coming to the club, dear? We're desperate for a fourth for mah-jong?'

'Vera, you old tart, fasten your top up when you're speaking to the boy,' Cindy chides. 'Max, I'll phone your mammy next week and make a date. Be sure and tell her to expect me!'

'And now, I think, the boy wants to go back into the water,' Dr Ahmed intercedes, and I gratefully escape to let the shimmering blue coolness hide my flaming face.

It goes without saying that my mother soon becomes firm friends with Vera and Cindy, and, together with a brusque, no-nonsense Forfar woman called Betty, they become the mah-jong team from hell, meeting up in each other's houses twice a week and playing in the club tournament every Tuesday. Alfie, our apprentice bearer, is permitted to serve them tea and cakes as his first solo mission, and passes with flying colours, only receiving censure for serving jam to guests out of the jar – which is how the family uses it – instead of decanting it into the new porcelain strawberry-shaped bowl bought specially for the purpose.

I, meanwhile, quickly come to terms with some of the odd little quirks of my new school which, though not an easy transition, has not been the sheer hell I've been fearing, and, with the exception of invoking the ire of some older teachers who were glad to see the back of the British at partition, I survive fairly well in a place where I'm, frankly, outnumbered two thousand to one.

Discipline is considered one of the most important virtues of our education here, and all of my teachers have their own individual methods of imposing it, which I discover to my cost in my first week, when I am obliged to spend an entire lesson with my arms in the air for forgetting a book; while being casually whacked with a heavy wooden ruler or belt by a passing teacher is considered the norm.

However, the offhand sadism of pernickety class teachers pales into insignificance when I meet the school's resident Doctor Fu Manchu, an inscrutable-faced Nepalese monk called Brother Pious who bears the somewhat ominous title of Overseer of Spiritual Well-being, and whose Reign of Terror lasts for almost the whole of my years at this new Alma Mater.

Our paths seem fated to cross on my first day, when, wandering slightly dazed through the maelstrom at morning recess, I stop to buy an ice lolly from a street vendor peddling his wares through the iron bars of the closed gate, and am just about to take my first lick when a hand slaps my sweet ice from my fingers and sends it skittering across the hot concrete of the playing field.

I swirl round ready to take on some chunky play-ground bully, but instead come face to face with a painfully thin man with an immobile sculpted face, his hooded snake eyes hidden behind dark green sun-glasses.

'Disease!' he hisses at me, although his lips appear not to move at all. 'These fellows bring disease, new boy! You have no ideas what creatures have made piss in the water that fellow used to make Popsicles! Go on with you now, go play!'

With what would prove to be his signature remark, the good brother vanishes with a swish of his immaculate white cassock, and I feel a hand on my shoulder as a friendly voice whispers, 'You bought from Outside. Murgia, man!'

I turn to behold a short, slightly pudding-faced, Chinese boy who I recognise as one of the teeming multitudes in my new class, and he clasps me firmly by the arm and leads me quickly away from the rapidly melting carcase of my lolly, muttering, 'We're for it if he catches us not playing any games. Come on, I'll show you where to go!'

'I don't understand,' I say tetchily. 'It's recess. I just wanted an ice cream!'

The boy laughs. 'Listen, you can only buy from the canteen during school time, and if Brother catches you going Outside you'll be thrashed. And we have to play games at recess, he'll know if we don't...'

'You've lost me,' I say exasperatedly and my new friend laughs again.

'Brother believes that laziness is a cardinal sin in Our Lady's eyes,' he says, quickly crossing himself before continuing, 'so he writes out a daily recess games rota for all the boys. We're on punching bags this week, but I was hiding because I can't reach and they all make fun of me. I thought he'd sniffed me out when he came over and I was dying, man, but then you came and saved me!'

'Think nothing of it,' I say dryly, and the boy laughs and offers his hand.

'Arnold Pang,' he says with a grin, 'you tell your daddy to bring you to our restaurant, my pop will make y'all something really special.'

CHAPTER 7

the curate's egg

Local bazaars hold a huge fascination for small boys, being cornucopias of endless forbidden delights like sticky sweetmeats and brightly-coloured firecrackers, both parentally classified as highly toxic. However, as a British child abroad, nipping out to the neighbourhood shops alone is considered completely outré, so one of the priorities for surviving as the junior member of a colonial household is to quickly enlist the aid of one or more servants as accomplices.

I had already singled out Mafzal, the driver, as a perfect accessory for illegal activities, but, as he was often otherwise engaged ferrying my mother and her buddies to and from various mah-jong games, it struck me as essential to recruit someone from the interior domestic staff as well, and, as I had been deemed too old to require the services of an ayah, I selected Alfie the bearer as my chosen right-hand man.

Alfie was lucky if he had celebrated his fifteenth birthday when he first came to us, despite his father's claims that he was eighteen and required a 'man's wage', and he proved to be a more than willing co-conspirator when it came to slipping out of the main gate and bringing me back rasgullâs while I distracted the pernickety cook on matters of supposed culinary importance.

However, the most desirable of the forbidden fruits available locally are fireworks, and Alfie is particularly adept at procuring some of the most unstable patakas ever manufactured from the bazaar shopkeepers on my behalf. Thus, on a warm afternoon in September, believing everyone to be safely out of the way, the young bearer and I have been filling old tin cans with illicitly-purchased bangers and then blowing them up in pyrotechnic cacophonies of noise, when we are rudely interrupted in our sport by the bleary-eyed figure of my father in his pyjama bottoms and singlet, bellowing, 'What the hell is going on out there!'

'Hai Rabba, it is the Manager Sahib,' Alfie whispers as we both dive for cover under the wide banana leaves of the lush fruit coppice. 'He has not yet returned to the mill. We are doomed, Chotta Sahib!'

'Well, we're certainly never going to see the light of day again if he finds out just who woke him up,' I say through pursed lips. 'Come on, if we hug the back wall we can get back into the house through the side door and pretend we've been in my room all along.'

However, just as we start to move, our escape route is blocked by a moustachioed durwan who arrives puffing on the scene, truncheon in hand, so Alfie motions me to follow him back into the shelter of the trees instead and leads the way to the servants' quarters at the rear of the house.

The door is padlocked shut, but Alfie fortunately has the single key in his pocket, and, hastily lifting the coarse hessian door-curtain we bolt into the safety of the narrow room that my accomplice shares with his boss, a clean but very basic cell which is furnished with two plain wooden beds and a simple armoire.

'Phew! You've saved us, Alfie,' I exhale, plopping down gratefully onto the cook's bed, which I notice now boasts the old horsehair mattress that had so horrified me on my first night away from Britain, and I realise that some deal has been brokered with the storeman who had come to remove it.

Alfie notes the line of my gaze, and, dropping onto his own hard bed, says in Urdu, with all the feigned innocence he can muster, 'Ah, it was Allah who saved us, Chotta Sahib, I am but his humble instrument and I do not complain, but it is a hard life indeed having to sleep upon these bare boards night after night, when a good servant to a fine Englishman such as your father needs to be alert and awake at all times...'

Outside I can hear the said 'fine Englishman' cursing out the durwan and demanding to know what bloody gundas have disturbed his afternoon siesta with their bloody firecrackers, and I look at my co-conspirator with a new-found respect.

'Gosh, you learn fast, Alfie,' I say admiringly. 'I will, of course, ask the Manager Sahib to have a mattress sent to you from the stores.'

'Chotta Sahib is too kind,' Alfie replies with only the faintest trace of a smirk.

Later that week we are all sitting at afternoon tea on what I have privately named Éclair Friday, this being the first day of the autumn that it has been deemed cool enough to purchase chocolate-covered choux pastries from the Savoy

Bakery in town, it being a feat of complex logistics to get these fragile confections from the shop to the house in quick enough time to stop the chocolate melting and the cream turning.

The said dainties have been sped home earlier this afternoon and refrigerated on arrival with a speed worthy of an organ transportation team, and have now been placed tentatively on the tea table, but their couverture tends to go liquid as soon they are picked up, and my father and I have been making a game of trying to swallow them whole, much to my mother's disgust, and we are still licking melted chocolate from our faces when she suddenly announces that we have all joined the church.

Out-of-the-blue pronouncements like this are fairly normal for my mother, but there is, nevertheless, a moment of stunned silence at this particular non sequitur. In fact, the hush is so deep that Alfie is in the process of sticking his head round the pantry doorway to check that we have not all dropped dead from excessive sugar consumption when Dad and I both start speaking at once.

'I have to go to ordinary school six days a week, I'm not going to have to go to Sunday school too, am I?' I protest, while my father grumbles, 'Church? There's only bloomin' left-footer churches around here. I'm not going to be seen in any papist chapel!'

My mother bangs her fist violently on the table, making all the crockery rattle and both Alfie and the cook stick their heads round the pantry door in anticipation of fireworks.

'You two are a pair of damn fools,' my mother complains. 'We are not becoming bally bishops, we are joining the church.'

My father looks at her sideways.

'There's something going on here, isn't there,' he says sceptically.

The preacher who heads the Christ Church, the town's only protestant chapel, is of the genial Church of England breed and, unlike the brothers at my school, would not look out of place in an old *Punch* cartoon singing the praises of his rotten egg. He is standing in front of his humble basilica, a mellow red-brick structure on a breezy hilltop location set amidst the only pines in the city, and he opens his arms in welcome as we climb out of the Vauxhall. It is a bright Saturday in early October, and my school has been granted a holiday to mark the death anniversary of some brutally slain holy man, thus robbing me of any excuse not to accompany my mother on our first appearance at this place of worship.

My dad has been seated at his breakfast as we depart, having returned from the mill after his morning stint as is his custom, and he remarks that we appear to be celebrating the Jewish Sabbath rather than the Christian one, but my mother ignores this jibe with a toss of her head. And, although I try to press her on the reasons for the Saturday visit in the car, her lips stay sealed like an obstinate clam, and I can extract nothing from her for the entirety of the hour-long journey.

'Hello, hello, you must be Rose, welcome, welcome to our little flock,' the vicar beams. 'I knew when you phoned yesterday that you would be as good as your word.

And is this young Max? My, what a big lad! He'll certainly be a real help with the tables.'

'Tables? What tables?' I ask my mother as the genial parson leads us to his church, but my mater simply digs me in the ribs and whispers, 'Shut up and keep smiling!'

The vicar, who is pretending he hasn't heard, opens the door and turns to us.

'Well, well, jolly good. Here we are then, God's little Saturday enterprise. Max, you come with me, and Rose, just you find Topsy, she'll point you in the right direction...'

My mother gives him her famous I'm-humouring-you-for-now smile and disappears, and, totally lost, I follow the genial parson towards a large cupboard.

'So nice of you to give up your holiday Saturday to come and help us out, Max. If you just grab an end of this table we'll take it through to the hall and I'll show you how to set up. It's terribly easy, you know, you'll soon pick it up.'

He indicates a folded trestle table and I just about manage to lift my end as the minister effortlessly lifts the other side and strides off, dragging me behind him, and we bustle into a room where several officious memsahibs in aprons, my mother amongst them, are piling the contents of large cardboard boxes onto already erected counters.

'Uncle,' I say tentatively, 'what exactly goes on here of a Saturday morning?'

'Neville, please, we're all equal servants in God's eyes,' he laughs. 'This is our weekly sale for Jesus, Max. People give us the stuff they want rid off and we sell it for them, and the church gets half the money.'

All around me I can see ancient items of clothing and some well-worn jigsaws and toys being loaded onto the rickety tables, most of it looking like the unsold leftovers of a jumble sale, and I marvel that anyone would bother to go through the effort of putting this kind of junk out for sale, let alone buy it.

'And do people actually come and buy this stuff?' I ask, incredulous.

'Oh yes, rather, when you've been here as long as I have, you get to hankering for something from Marks and Spencer now and then, and it's always a nice feeling to find something from home. Then there's the indigenous population too. They all love it, makes them think they're pucka sahibs if they can wear something that came from old Saint Michael in the Blighty!'

'But hasn't it ... well ... had its day, most of it?'

Neville laughs. 'Oh yes, lots of it has. But we get good stuff too. There's queues right down the hill some Saturdays when the word gets out that a burrah sahib's leaving and selling up his worldlies!'

'Ah,' I say, realisation beginning to dawn, 'and do the helpers get first pick?'

'Perk of the job, dear boy,' Neville replies. 'God always helps his helpers.'

My holiday Saturday starts to go downhill when we leave the church and Mother announces that we are picking up Harriet and Elsa, the twins, from their military cadet training centre and taking them back to our house for lunch.

'Has the cook prepared anything special or will the twins just kill a passing goat and eat it raw?' I ask sulkily, envisaging my planned afternoon with the dog-eared Famous Five novel I have just purchased now spent watching the unchecked ethnic cleansing of our bungalow's ornithological population instead, but my mother just treats me to one of her extra-special dirty looks.

'Can't you be bally civil for just one afternoon? Those girls both love you so much, and I do like young Harriet, she's so nice and well mannered.'

'Well mannered?' I splutter. 'You mean she remembers to say please and thank you to everything they slaughter?'

'Oh, you're just a narrow-minded old fool like your father and Wallace. You'd just sit on the damn veranda with your nose in some bally book if I let you. At least the twins like to run about and play!'

'Play?' I think to myself. 'You call that mass genocide playing? If they were back in Dundee they'd have season tickets for the children's panel,' but further conjecture on the vagaries of fate is cut short by Mafzal pulling the car up in front of a large military-style building and the twins bounding out from the shady pool of its vast imperial doorway.

'Hello, hello, Aunty, where have you been? Aunty, we're so-oo hungry. Can we stop at the cheena bedamm store on the way home? Pleeease, Aunty?' they wheedle, plying my mother with hugs and kisses, and I have to concede that their technique is flawless, as my normally strict mother melts like ghee on a chapatti griddle and instructs the driver to stop at the next roadside shop to purchase Bombay mix for our guests.

Sensing a potential paan break, Mafzal needs no persuading, and we screech out of the cantonment's palm-lined driveway and out onto the main road in a matter of seconds, quickly parking in front of a small bazaar where open-fronted shops offer every kind of fast food imaginable.

'Stay close to Mafzal, children, and don't buy anything that's uncovered, and no water ices,' my mother chides, doling out a rupee to each of us, and, revelling in our unaccustomed liberty, we all head for the stalls without a backward glance.

The twins are soon engaged in an intricate bargaining ritual with a piaju-wallah who is clearly out of his depth and looks in imminent danger of being bankrupted on the spot, while I sidle over to Mafzal who is eyeing the paan vendor's stall with longing in his eyes.

'Our usual arrangement, Chotta Sahib?' the driver says through closed lips and I nod, handing over my rupee note and telling the stall keeper to give my driver two annas' worth of the drug of his choice.

'Tell me, Chotta Sahib,' Mafzal enquires, slipping his leafy green cone stuffed with succulent spices into his mouth as I pocket my change, 'what is the fascination of so many books and comics?'

'Ah, Mafzal,' I reply, 'I wish I knew!'

Before coming to Pakistan I had never been much of a bookworm, being a typical British child who existed on an unadulterated diet of television comedy and *The Beano*. However, when confronted with a world where TV did not exist and radio was but a watery connection to the BBC World Service, I had suddenly discovered a voracious appetite for the written word, and had become busily engaged in making up for eleven years' worth of lost time.

Our school library, such as it was, fought a losing battle in meeting the needs of two thousand boys with long afternoons to fill, and everything in its catalogue from the wormholed pre-partition editions of *Beau Geste* to the much fought-over Hardy Boys paperbacks were pored over on a daily basis.

I soon learned that the accepted way to procure the best reads was to show up at seven-thirty in the morning and join the wolf pack that hovered behind 'Library Sir' when he made his rounds for the day, placing the previous afternoon's returns back on the shelves, and there were regular scrums each morning for the coveted tomes of Franklin W Dixon and Enid Blyton.

The only other option for bibliophiles was to head for the many book stores in the 'new market' where American comic books and hundreds of Russian titles translated into dodgy English could be purchased, but, as was the case with all imported goods, there was a steep price tag to be contended with, and ten rupees a month pocket money did little damage in a world where an *Archie* comic – if you could find one – cost a rupee, and a novel would set you back two or three rupees fifty.

However, my mother also made me a daily food allowance of one rupee to spend at the school canteen, and I soon learned how to get by on a two-anna cup of the local chai – a strangely refreshing concoction made of strong tea and condensed milk – each morning and keep the rest of the cash to spend at one of the many second-hand book stalls that lined the south end of the town's main road.

These eccentric street emporiums, where dog-eared copies of James Bond novels jostled for shelf space with books of Islamic theology and portraits of Bollywood stars, were little more than tin-roofed garden sheds, but they were the real life blood of the city's reading public and I was soon rubbing shoulders with Chittagong's teeming throngs each day, selecting reading material for the hour-long drive home and the hot afternoon to come.

A used comic cost just four annas, a book eight, and after my tea and the customary two anna paan-bribe for Mafzal's compliance, my daily food rupee still left me twelve annas to spend on the deliciously diverse literature that found its way to the stalls.

Thus, standing by the busy paan stand with Mafzal, I watch the twins extracting about five rupees worth of fried bhaji from the hapless piaju-wallah, and figure that they'll fill the car with so much aroma and noise that my mother will never notice that I've pocketed my food cash. Content with a job well done, I follow them back to the car, when the belligerent Elsa suddenly turns to me and points.

'Hey, look at those bastards over there with that mangy dog. I bet they're going to drown the bugger. Hey, you fellows, can we watch you kill it?!'

I whirl to see two middle-class Anglo-Indian boys of about fifteen, wearing closed-in leather shoes and dressed in cotton slacks and smart silk shirts. This apparel is not so very extraordinary in itself, although more common on a Sunday, perhaps, but what really marks them as unusual is that despite their Sunday-best get-ups the taller of the two is carrying a small brown and white pye puppy in his arms.

Hearing Elsa's guttural mutterings and spotting the carload of white people they come over, hands extended in greeting, and the puppy meets my gaze with his big limpid pools and I know that I am lost and have to have him, regardless of what I will have to give up in exchange.

'Hello, hello, y'all, how are you today, my friends,' the elder one gushes, the smell of his brilliantine quite overpowering in the afternoon heat. 'I am Darrel and this is my brother Clive. You are a fellow pupil of St Peter's, are you not, young man? I have seen you running from Brother Pious at recess. Come, come. You wish to come to visit our home? My mama will be honoured to welcome you all!'

'What you doing with that damn dog, man?' Elsa enquires, brushing their polite overtures aside. 'You going to drown the bugger?'

Darrel looks at her askance. 'What you think we are, man? Savages? We were taking him to the bishop's house to give to an old Bengali woman but she's gone and died so we're bringing him home again. Aunty, do you want this dog for your young fellow here? I have seen this poor fellow at school, Aunty, he has no friends other than one fat Chinese bugger, get him a good dog and cheer him up some.'

I look to Harriet, my mother's current favourite, praying that she'll weigh in and fight my corner for me, but things are already in the hands of a greater power. The pup and my mother have made eye contact and she is completely in its thrall.

I have a dog.

I have just bought *Five Go to Mystery Moor*, where Enid Blyton's sexually ambivalent boarding-school sleuths effortlessly defeat a pack of evil gypsies within the six-week confines of their summer 'hols', and it firmly preordains that my new dog can be called nothing other than Timmy after his more famous canine counterpart.

Mafzal grumbles that the damn animal will bring fleas and parasites into the pristine interior of his car, but I tell him sotto voce that as we already have the twins in situ things can't get much worse, and he is so amused at my irreverence that he completely forgets to be grouchy about the dog. My father, likewise, goes through the motions of grumbling about 'bloody pot-lickers' but is also soon under the puppy's spell, and, all in all, it takes less than an hour for Timmy the wonder dog to become completely integrated into our humble household.

Me and Timmy

it's a wonderful life

The year is unravelling with sickening rapidity and the end of term is suddenly just round the corner. The Pakistani school year follows the calendar rather than British academic tradition, and final exams are suddenly taking up a lot of my time. I'm breezing through English and arithmetic, but the unfamiliar terrains of the local history are proving to be an uphill slog, and I spend most evenings with my books trying to cram the progress of Alexander the Great across Asia into my protesting brain.

Early mornings have become slightly chilly, a fact borne out by the sight of hundreds of boys all huddled in the sunny patches of the playground before school each day, and whereas it's still hot enough to spend my afternoons at the pool, I'm now finding myself having to abandon the water by about four and venture into the forbidden territory of my mother's afternoon mah-jong sessions.

Today is the Chittagong Club's ladies' weekly mah-jong tournament, and towelling my goose-pimpled flesh dry, I quickly dress and head up to the main club-house that overlooks the pool from its hilltop position. The original Edwardian building sits regally here on the site of a former tea garden, oblivious to its own anachronistic British mock-Tudor architecture, and I walk tentatively through its deserted verandas in search of my mother and her friends.

A soft click-click noise tells me that a couple of old sahibs are still in the billiard room finishing up lunchtime's game, and two leather-faced drunks are propping up the bar and ruminating on the good old days, but of the mah-jong-until-death crowd there is no sign. Bemused, I wander into the shuttered ballroom in the hope of locating them there, but here I find only cockroaches and the ghosts of long-past parties, and I about jump out of my skin when an old bearer comes up behind me on silent feet and asks who I seek.

'The Mah-jong Memsahibs, Chotta Sahib?' he says with a nervous grin. 'I would not be disturbing those ladies at this time of the day. They are all in the bioscope hall, but I beg you, do not go inside, Sahib, wait in the foyer where there are soft chairs and the British *Daily Mirror*. That will be much safer.'

He vanishes as quietly as he has come, and, blinking as I go back out into the daylight, I retrace my steps and pad down a long corridor past the card room and into the dim foyer of the club's largest function hall. There's an alien scent of stale beer here from the previous night's tamasha, and a stack of trestle tables waits for the ladies to finish their games and make way for whatever festivity is planned for the evening. However, there are, as promised, some old cracked-leather armchairs and a bound copy of the *Overseas Daily Mirror* for the first week of August, 1965, and, flipping through the pages to find Andy Capp, I settle down to wait for my mother and her team of dreadnoughts.

In its native China the game of mah-jong is a popular pastime with both sexes, but in Indo-Pakistan it's a strictly ladies-only blood sport, and I can clearly hear the slightly shrill murmur of feline voices and the regular rumble of shuffling tiles as I sit waiting for them to finish for the day. Some ladies play 'friendly' mah-jong, but my mother's crowd are in it solely for the hard cash and the merciless crushing of their opponents, and the weekly club session is a sort of medieval jousting tournament where the winners from each table of four players move up a notch each round until the day's final session, when the four highest scorers face each other over the ivory tiles in a fight to the death to claim the afternoon's cash pot.

There's suddenly an extra-loud shuffling of tiles accompanied by the scraping of metal and wicker chairs on the hall's marble floor, and the heavy double doors swing open like a flood-gate and a torrent of women bursts into the dark lobby like a tsunami. There are old white women in dated cinch-waisted frocks linked arm in arm with dowager-like ladies in rainbow-hued saris; nattily dressed young Pakistani women in saffron and sapphire chatting to mini-skirted Europeans; and then my mother's crowd, loud gaudy mill memsahibs with too much rouge and lipstick, lighting up cigarettes and cackling over their afternoon's victory.

'Oooo, look! There's Max,' Vera of the slippery bikini-top coos as my mother's party spots my hiding place, 'Look, he's sitting all alone with the Blighty papers, he must have found some nudey girls to look at!'

'He's far too young for all that bally nonsense,' my mother says, I hope in my defence. 'He's just reading one of his damn books while he waits for us.'

'Hiyah, sweetie,' the ginger-haired Cindy winks to me, 'you best stay in your mammy's good books tonight. She's just been up against the Kraut table for today's pot and wiped the floor with them all!'

'It was Normandy all over again,' Vera chips in. 'You should have seen her making them squeal!'

'Yeah, she flattened them like a Panzer tank. Went straight in with the Four Winds and finished the game without a survivor in sight!'

'Be quiet, you bally idiots,' my mother chides. 'They're coming out...'

Vera suppresses a snort of laughter as three very large ladies, who look like Wagnerian valkyries sans their horned helmets, goose-step out of the hall and turn as one to face my mother's party.

'That was an exhilarating tournament,' the leader barks. 'We will have the return match next week, no?'

'Oh, we're counting off the hours,' Cindy replies with an almost straight face and the Teutons depart stiffly to Vera's smothered laughter.

'Hell, we showed them, girls,' she laughs, ruffling my still damp hair. 'Come on, Max. Let's go and buy cakes. Your mother's paying!'

As the end of the school year approaches Sir Lester announces that we must each bring in five rupees to pay for the annual class picnic, and, after much grumbling from my mother, the said cash is advanced and I am told to report to the churchyard at five in the morning on the last Saturday of term.

Mafzal laughs when I tell him this and says that no one will actually come to the school at that hour, and that we can safely show up around six-thirty, but I am insistent that I must be present at the prescribed time and we duly turn up at the church in swirling mists and the eerie half-light of dawn.

'Enjoy your wait, Chotta Sahib,' Mafzal laughs as he drives away, and I look uncertainly around me at the quiet church and mist-shrouded cemetery as his tail lights vanish on the horizon.

Some workmen have been doing their annual maintenance on the large crucifix that marks the centre of the normally restful cemetery, and the contorted figure of Christ has been taken down and lies on the grass by me, carelessly covered in sacking, and I shudder as I see his bleeding hand protruding from one side of the coarse cloth.

Normally an area of bustle and noise, at dawn the churchyard is unnaturally hushed with only the soft cawing of distant crows singing a melancholy chorus, and I settle down uneasily in the chapel doorway and wrap my thin jumper tightly around me as I wait patiently for my teacher and classmates to arrive.

Twenty minutes slide slowly past, and huddled against the church door for warmth, I start to slowly drift off to sleep, only to be jolted awake with a cry a few moments later as a ghostly figure seems to float out of the mist towards me.

'Hai Rabba, man! You scared the hell out of me shrieking like that,' the voice of my friend, Arnold Pang, echoes through the mist. 'I was sure it was the statue of our Lord resurrected!'

People begin to show up around six, and, true to Mafzal's prediction, Sir Lester arrives on the half hour on the back of a large truck complete with an armed durwan, two cooks and a large bamboo cage full of about twenty squawking chickens.

'Why have they brought chickens?' I ask naively and Arnold makes a throat-cutting gesture.

'five-rupee picnic, man,' he laughs, and I am standing there open-mouthed trying to come up with a suitably scathing retort when Sir calls everyone to order and packs us all onto the back of the lorry.

'Boys, I have been privileged to have had the pleasure of your company for the last year,' our teacher orates passionately, 'and I hope that you will all bring honour to my name next year with your new class teachers. But today is not about work and study, today is about camaraderie and playing games, and I have invited a very special friend on our excursion this morning to make that happen. Let's all give him a big class welcome!'

We all cheer loudly, expecting anyone from a Bollywood film star to a local athlete, but the roar dies in our throats as a thin and wiry figure emerges out of the remnants of the mist and hoists himself onto our truck.

'Where are your manners, boys?' Sir Lester chides, 'Say good morning to Brother Pious.'

The heavy truck drives off softly through the early morning streets of the town, past fruit vendors hanging large necklaces of fat dried figs on their stalls, and then out along the still-misty river road where women stand in the swirling waters washing clothes and filling copper urns. Brother is in good spirits and, patting backs as he goes, works his way to the cab end of the truck, where, amidst the chickens, an old wind-up Victrola has been hooked up to a large metal Tannoy speaker, and, taking the mike, the normally feared priest leads us all in singing the Pakistan national anthem and then various patriotic chants, the favourite of which goes with a handclap, thus – 'Pak, Pak, Pakistan! Zinzabad!'

Up until now I have been rather out of my depth with the whole concept of this Victorian-style formal picnic complete with servants and large cooked meals, but now, riding along the side of the muddy brown river with the wind in my hair, chanting and singing with my friends, I can think of no place on earth that I would rather be. The countryside gets lusher and greener as we speed along the bumpy road, each jolt promoting a cheer from the boys as we are flung this way and that, and, with the town well behind us, Sir Lester takes the mike and leads us all in song, his fine bass voice crooning 'You Ain't Nuttin' but a Hound Dawg' far better than any Elvis-impersonator could ever aspire to.

We have been granted leave to picnic on a semi-derelict private estate, originally the home of the local potentate in pre-Brit days, and we drive through large dilapidated gates guarded by rusty cannons and into a not inconsiderable field surrounded by a grove of mango trees and denser jungle beyond. The durwan takes up his position at the edge of the forest, shotgun in hand, while the cooks set about building fires, and soon have great pots of breakfast eggs boiling on their impromptu stoves.

Brother Pious calls me to his side and together we pace out the boundaries of a cricket pitch, and it isn't long before we have all been divided into teams and a spirited game has commenced, with Arnold and myself somehow contriving to field in the furthest outlying positions possible, skulking under the leafy shade of the bordering fruit trees.

'Are there animals out here, Arnold?' I ask, indicating the gun-toting durwan with a jerk of my head, but my friend only laughs.

'You're watching too many movies, man. There's nothing here but mosquitoes. Sir's more worried about us all being robbed. These old places are riddled with bandit camps.'

'Do you think they'll be serving breakfast soon?' I ask, swallowing the lump in my throat.

With the possible exception of the chickens, everyone present has the greatest day of their lives, and even Brother Pious' constant umpiring can do nothing to dampen our enthusiasm and energy. Cricket finally ceases when the cooks serve up a huge meal at about half past one, and we all retire to the shade with our tin plates and mugs of chai, tucking into spicy meat and dhal with heaps of rice and freshly-rolled chapattis.

Everyone settles down to rest after dinner, as even the winter sun is too hot to run about in, but we venture out at about three to what is known locally as a tank, being an ornate walled-in pond, and we step tentatively down its algaed marble steps to bathe in the lily-strewn water.

I'm floating contentedly in the cool green liquid, the mingled scent of flowers and sandalwood soap in my nostrils, when Sir comes down the steps to join me. He's quite a formidable sight in just a lunghi that does little to conceal his substantial pot belly, and I avert my eyes tactfully as he settles down in the water beside me.

'So, my friend,' he says kindly, 'you have survived your first class, even if your knowledge of our history still needs a lot more study. Tell me, how have you found it?'

I have a bellyful of some of the best food that I have ever eaten and have actually enjoyed playing cricket with my friends. I am sitting in a beautiful pond on carved stone steps that predate my ancestors setting foot in this remarkable country and I am looking forward to Christmas, a parcel of books from Britain and a month's holiday to read them in. There is no other answer that I can give.

'Amazing, Sir,' I say quietly, 'quite amazing.'

Dad in the back garden of
our house in Chittagong

CHAPTER 9

ᴩᴿᴏᴩꜱᴿ ᴄʜᴿɪꜱᴛᴍᴀꜱ

The December skies dawn blue-white and cloudless, and though the Yuletide evenings are cool and mosquito-ridden the days remain pleasant and sunny. Some men from the mill arrive to install a framework of strange wooden poles around my bed, and a heavy net tent is hung from it to repel the worst of the night vampires, but some still manage to get in and my arms are soon covered with ugly red bumps. Timmy, my dog, manages to burst the fragile contraption on its first morning, dashing into my room and leaping onto my bed, ripping the fragile net like a circus dog jumping through a paper hoop, and spidery darns grace my nights for the rest of the winter.

A boat has arrived from Britain bringing a parcel of Christmas goodies from my sister plus rolls of British newspapers from my dad's cousin, Bunty, and these strange heavy cylinders of print soon become a commodity more precious than gold in our little expat community.

My dad quickly trades his four-month-old copies of *The Sunday Post* with Wallace for some equally aged *News of the Worlds*, and even I manage to do a deal for a stack of *Archie* comic books with some American missionary's children in exchange for last summer's *Beanos*, and, all in all the papers end up doing the rounds of the entire jute wallahs' camp.

Christmas trees are also rarer than gold dust here, the only ones in the shops in town being strange velvet contraptions that look like assemblages of fat green cigars with beads on the ends of them, and, there being no handy young conifers to chop down, the vicar at the Christ Church doles out branches from his sparse firs in a seasonal lottery, with Heath-Robinsonlike contraptions standing shakily in impromptu crêpe-paper-covered pots quickly gracing the houses of the chosen few.

A junior manager in my dad's employ offers his services to me as a tree-building engineer, and arrives at the house three days before Christmas Eve with a large artificial spruce, laboriously constructed out of wire and meticulously hand-cut paper, the boughs incongruously finished with bright paper flowers. My mother rolls her eyes at this perceived ethnic eccentricity, but I find the floral conifer quite fetching, and, as it turns out, our display is much envied by all over the next couple of weeks.

Decorations are, likewise, hard to find and expensive to purchase, so I press Alfie and Mafzal into service, and we make yards and yards of brightly-coloured paper chains and bunting out of the fragile glassine paper that street children use to make kites, and we quickly festoon the house and verandas to mark the occasion.

No one has received any Christmas cards from Blighty as yet, the estimated time of delivery being February or March, but locally produced cards depicting Asian artists' visions of Olde England in the snow begin to circulate, and the window-sills quickly fill with greetings from the locality. However, just days before the big event, a thin blue aerogramme does arrive from Dundee, containing Aunty Barbara's secret recipe for clootie dumpling, and the cook immediately sets to work with raisins and suet, sweltering over his hot coal-fired range as the massive pudding bubbles and spits for hours on end.

It seems strange to be sitting down to a traditional British Christmas dinner on a hot sunny day, but the British in India have never had any problem with building Little Englands wherever they go, and we duly work our way through oxtail soup, turkey and then Christmas pudding, the festivity completed with crackers made from crêpe paper and old toilet rolls with bazaar-bought plastic toys and homemade paper hats.

We have all been down to the new market to purchase gifts, and I have bought locally produced cologne for my mother, which she promptly decants into an old designer bottle so that she can lord it over her friends, while my father is ecstatic with his HP Sauce, a delicacy costing an exorbitant eighteen rupees a bottle from the classiest grocer in town. Mafzal is easy to please, and I get him paan and cigarettes, whilst Alfie presents more of a challenge, but I eventually settle on a fountain pen which I have gold-engraved with his nickname.

After the bustle of the school year the festive season proves to be quite solitary for me, and I spend most of my holiday with only the dog and Enid Blyton for company, although my mother, determined to cure me of my bookish habits, packs me off to the church Christmas party on Boxing Day. However, this occasion proves to be nothing short of embarrassing as I am a foot and a half taller than the biggest child there, and, after spending the afternoon helping the genial Neville hand out glasses of orange squash, I retreat happily back into the world of literature for the remainder of my vacation.

In dire need of a fix of her own after almost a week of abstinence, my mother invites her mah-jong buddies round to the house on the first day that my dad returns to the mill, and I am summarily shunted from my customary seat on the back veranda to make way for their gaming table and chairs. Not to be outdone, the dog and I move three yards along the deck and simply settle on the cool marble of the veranda floor, and I am smugly engrossed in *The Mystery of the Spiteful Letters* when I'm smartly outmanoeuvred by the sound of loud farts from the ladies' table.

I look up, aghast, but play seems to be continuing normally behind the walls of ivory tiles, and the culprit, the grey-haired Vera, merely shrugs and mutters, 'Bit of tummy trouble, girls,' as she sprays a dash of perfume into the air before continuing with her hand.

'Vera! You're ruining feminine mystique for Max before he's even pinched a bum for himself,' the red-haired Cindy reproaches with a grin.

'Well, he can come and pinch mine any time he likes,' Vera replies diffidently, wiggling her posterior on her seat. 'Just you come and grab yourself a handful, Max!'

'I think I'll go just and play with the dog,' I mutter into my socks, stashing my book and vanishing quickly into the garden to the sound of their giggles.

Defeated, I get Mafzal to take Timmy and myself down to the local beach, a huge stretch of muddy sand about ten miles down the road that's strewn with driftwood and other refuse churned up by the winter tides. It's reached by bumping down an unsignposted narrow lane that turns abruptly from tarmac to dirt track and then just stops by the unending shore, and there is nothing to see for miles but the brownish ocean and a solitary kutcha shop selling forbidden snack food and some bizarre shell ornaments.

Mafzal glances longingly at their display of paan, but we're both flat broke after the holiday so we walk on by and let the dog off his leash, running along the clay-laden sands with him till both canine and humans are giddy with exhaustion.

Slinking back into the house at about half past four, I'm planning on polishing off whatever cake and sandwiches the mah-jong crowd have left and then finishing my book, but as I slip noiselessly through the French windows I find my dad seated in his armchair with a very tall, well-dressed, dark-skinned man wearing imported clothes and a rather dashing silk tie.

'At last,' my dad says, exasperated, as if making conversation with this unfamiliar man has been an effort. 'Max, this is Donald Cameron from the British Council.'

The said Donald Cameron jumps up from his seat and thrusts an unexpectedly calloused hand in my direction. 'Dashed pleased to meet you, old boy!' he gushes in an accent that sounds like a Pakistani Nigel Pargeter. 'We're always really pleased to see pucka new faces like yours here amongst the jolly old sahibs!'

I shoot my dad a what's-Mum-volunteered-me-for-now look as Donald continues to vigorously shake my hand, and, taking pity on me, my father intercedes.

'Donald's from the Information Unit of the Council,' he tells me slowly, 'they're putting on a film show for us tonight. I thought you'd like to help him set up.'

The pieces fall suddenly into place and I see the big picture, and, clasping the big man's hand in a suddenly enthusiastic grip, I reply, 'Of course, when do we start?'

Between our house and the mill there's a stretch of formal garden and a low-rise block of flats where the junior assistants and under-managers have their quarters, and it is here that Donald has chosen for tonight's show. There has been no formal announcement that anything is planned, but when we pull up in his liveried Land Rover there is already a small crowd gathered on the burrah maidan, and the place is packed with eager workers waiting patiently for the 'Belite bioscope' long before twilight.

Donald parks the Land Rover on the grass next to a dense clump of trees, and, under his direction, we erect a large tubular steel frame onto one side of it, then stretch a heavy pearlescent screen across its length. It looks fairly saggy to begin with, but the friendly projectionist shows me how to tighten thin leather straps like bootlaces though the brass eyelets on the screen's black edge, and, after a good half hour spent tugging on the spidery strands, we finally have an absolutely smooth surface.

'Tiptop, old chap,' my new friend says, nodding with satisfaction, 'now let's have a look and see what jolly old gems we've got to show them all tonight.'

He opens the back of the vehicle to reveal a monstrous old sixteen-millimetre projector that looks like it was conscripted to show movies to the troops during the War of the Roses, and several trunks packed full of films in rusty metal cans.

'Ah, yes, some cartoons,' Donald mutters, more to himself than to me, 'and what's this? *How to Use Your Morrison Shelter*. Nope, don't see that one going down too well with the mill gundas... ah-ha! Here's the chap we want, *Princess Margaret's Wedding* in Technicolor, that's always a hit!'

'How many films do you have in here, Donald?' I ask, peering curiously into the stack of dusty trunks.

'No one knows,' he says simply, 'that's the beauty of working for Queen and country and all that, we never throw any of our films away and the ones that other units don't want they send to us. I think there's one of the Relief of Mafeking in here somewhere.'

It's dark by seven o'clock and everyone shuffles down to the green for the show. Unlike Wallace, my dad dislikes playing royalty at these events, and my mother squeezes onto a sofa with the local wives while he inconspicuously joins the Captain on the hard chairs at the rear. I've been dreading being similarly regulated to the back of the open air auditorium, but there's a gaggle of kids sitting cross-legged on the grass and I spy Tono, the Captain's son, amongst them and quickly go to join him before anyone can spot me as being too tall for the front row.

Donald starts up the old projector, and a beam like a searchlight shoots out across the grass, throwing the silhouettes of moths onto the silver screen as a scratchy union jack appears to the muffled soundtrack of the national anthem, and the words 'Crown Film Unit' come into view.

Hundreds of mill workers have shown up for the bioscope show, and what they make of *The Danger of Nuclear Attack* and *The 1959 Edinburgh Military Tattoo* is anybody's guess, but there's always an enthusiastic cheer as each bumpy old short comes to an end, and when the last Halas and Batchelor wartime propaganda cartoon concludes at nine o'clock there's a sigh of disappointment as Donald turns the projector off.

The January night air has turned decidedly chilly and we children have long since formed into a huddle under an old travelling rug, and our mothers have likewise bunched together on their sofas for warmth. Sensing the end of the evening's entertainment the mill workers begin to disband and drift back to the coolie lines behind the factory buildings, talking in soft voices about the wonders of foreign lands, and the Captain invites the upper pecking-order families to partake of tea and hot singaras in his house before everyone retires to bed.

Donald has declined the Captain's hospitality and has already dismantled the large screen and packed his movies back into the Land Rover, and I go over to bid my new friend farewell before he departs.

'When will you be back?' I ask, shaking his huge hand, and he ruffles my hair in parting and smiles.

'Who knows, old chap, I go where the wild wind blows. I'm in the jungle next week and then up to the Hill Tracts, but if I can get back down before the rains come I'll pop in to see you all again. Toodle pip for now, Muffin!'

Hot weather in Chittagong —
me and Mum on a typical
Chittagong bench made from
old chairs

waiting for rain

Being separated from your friends when you are assigned to a new class at the start of the school year is a major fear amongst my peers, and Arnold and I stand listening to the roll call with trepidation on our first day back. However, the gods appear to be momentarily on our side, and we are both placed into the same class again, this time under the tutelage of a no-nonsense French-Canadian monk called Brother Jean-Paul.

A militant artist in an establishment where little time is granted to creative pursuits, Brother Jean-Paul must receive a lot of the credit for making me who I am today, but though I looked forward to his lessons daily, my school year was counter-balanced by a tall pinched-face teacher called Sir Jeremy, who appeared to have been put on earth for the sole purpose of making my life a misery.

Many of the stricter teachers at St Peter's had reputations which preceded them, but Sir Jeremy came as a complete surprise, and the first inkling I had that he was to be avoided was when he walked into our classroom and Arnold whispered, 'Murgia! This fellow is bad news, man.'

'What's wrong with him?' I whisper back, but before Arnold can reply the teacher's X-ray vision sears across the crowded classroom as he shouts, 'You there, yes you, Mr Ching-Chong-Chinaman, you have something to say?

Maybe you want to come up here and talk to my class for me? Oh, and what's this I see? There's an *Englishman* beside you. Oh yes, I know your type, Mr Huntley and Palmer's Biscuit Wallah. You also want to take over my class, do you not? Well you fellows can no longer wield your power, because let me tell you, British rule is well over, man, and there's no telling me how to eat my English biscuits anymore, so be warned, this is not the Merry Sherwood Forest and I will make your life hell for this year. You follow me? Hell. H-E-L-L!'

There's a ripple of nervous laughter from the boys which evaporates as quickly as it starts, as Sir Jeremy strides briskly down the centre of the room and brings a heavy wooden ruler down across my desk with a resounding thwack.

'You follow, Biscuit Wallah?' he smirks at me, 'I am going to make your life hell!'

Sir Jeremy's classes soon become gladiatorial arenas for the rest of the boys to sit back and watch each day's massacre, and I find myself praying that some other unfortunate will inadvertently annoy him and become the focus of his considerable ire, but it is to no avail, and though our persecution is by no means exclusive, Arnold and I seem destined to be the star turns in the ritual slaughtering that masquerades as our education under this sneering instructor.

One of his favourite games is to pretend to be deaf, so that when I have to answer a question he will cup one hand to his ear and say, 'I cannot hear you, Biscuit Wallah, you are not in Piccadilly London now, my friend, speak so that real men can hear your tea and biscuits voice,' and, if I am stupid enough to rise to the bait and raise my voice, he will yell my answer back at me in a squeaky impersonation of a British accent, much to the amusement of the rest of the class.

It has to be said, however, that no matter how intensely annoying Sir Jeremy is, he is usually more irritating than actually harmful, and that the gym master is far more dangerous when to comes to the possibility of random physical violence, but his endless verbal antics set the scene perfectly for what proves to be God's ultimate practical joke one Monday morning in late February.

I have contracted a miscellaneous tropical fever and have been absent from school for over a week, leaving Arnold alone to bear the brunt of endless chicken-chow-mein jibes from our favourite tormentor, and when I am finally pronounced fit by our jovial mill doctor – a dead ringer for Peter Sellers in *The Millionairess* – I'm left dyspeptic and constipated by the after-effects of the virus.

The good doctor duly prescribes a strong laxative, which for some inexplicable reason, my mother doles out to me at breakfast on my first day back at school, and I'm sitting in Sir Jeremy's class room for the first lesson of the day when things abruptly begin to move in my bowels. I try to sit it out till the end of the lesson, but after three minutes I know that this is just not going to be possible, and, sweat pouring down my brow, I leave my seat and walk up to my teacher like Oliver Twist with his empty gruel bowl.

'You crazy, man?!' Arnold whispers frantically, clutching at my sleeve, but I am a desperate child and nothing can stop me, and I walk straight up to my nemesis and baldly declare, 'I have to go to the toilet, Sir.'

Sir Jeremy turns from writing on his blackboard and looks down at me, a sneer of delight all over his pinched little face.

'What's that, Biscuit Wallah, you want to go to the bathroom? This is class time, man, you can't go piss now. Go at recess,' he says dismissively, turning back to the board.

'You don't understand,' I say back, as calmly as is possible in the given circumstances, 'I have to go, now!'

Jeremy turns, his face saying that this is going to be better than he even dared imagine, before he utters the one word that I have been dreading.

'Why?'

I'm standing, by now hopping from foot to foot, in front of sixty twelve-year-old boys with essence of Senna-pod burning its way through my gut at an alarming rate, and I have, literally, no time left to play this irritating teacher's tedious parlour games, so, in a loud clear voice I say, 'Sir, I have taken a laxative and I need to go to the toilet, now!'

The class explodes with laughter, and I can hear Arnold's muttered 'Murgia!' as his head hits the desk, but surprisingly Sir Jeremy chooses not to milk the situation any further, and, indicating the open door with his head, he makes a dismissive gesture and I run gratefully from the room.

I fly down several flights of concrete stairs and make my way to the toilets at the back of the school, a place which I have skilfully avoided using up to date. The rickety outhouse is about the size of a British suburban garage with an open front, and it has been economically constructed out of steel girders and finished with a pitched corrugated-iron roof and three-quarter-height plaster walls topped with chicken-wire above eye level.

It's before nine in the morning and the day hasn't heated up yet, yet the stink is already unbearable, but I'm being driven by circumstances far beyond my control, and, taking a deep breath, I venture quickly inside.

There are two rows of stalls, and, matters being somewhat pressing, I bolt into the nearest one and close the door, looking with horror at the crude facilities before me. The toilet itself is just an elliptical hole in the ground that leads to a rudimentary clay pipe – stained dark brown from years of use – that in turn leads to the cesspit below, and the stench of sewer gas makes me want to retch. The floor is already wet and dirty, but someone has obligingly put two bricks at either side of the hole for users to place their feet while they squat, and closing my eyes, I quickly drop my trousers and assume the position.

It least it can't get any worse now, I think, balancing precariously on the wobbly blocks, unaware that God has one final trick left up his sleeve, and as I open my eyes to leave, I see that there is no toilet paper and that only an old ghee tin half full of water has been provided for the purpose of cleaning up.

One of the things I had loved most about India was the constant parade of Hindu pujas throughout the year, and some of my earliest memories are of my ayah taking me to see the fantastic oil-lamp-lit effigies of multi-armed gods and goddesses in their magnificent stage sets in the homes of wealthy Indians.

I can still vividly remember standing transfixed before a huge fabric and papier mâché diorama where the brightly-painted clay goddess Durga towered regal over an unfortunate peasant about to be devoured by a lion; her ten arms pointing to her equally fascinating children, especially the elephant-headed Ganesh, and making my poor ayah tell me the story of the Hindu holy family time and time again.

However, if Durga Puja was the staple food of an imaginative small child, then Diwali and the wor-shipping of the savage blue goddess, Kali, was a veritable banquet. I'm told that I became totally insufferable during Diwali and could only be quietened when in the presence of the fifteen-foot-high goddess herself, her tongue stuck out defiantly as she stood on the bloodied corpse of a slain enemy, a necklace of heads around her neck, her ten arms often clutching machetes and stranglers' cords.

Friendly contractors and mill under-managers were quick to provide invitations to their pujas to the Manager Sahib's eager boy, and I was bedecked in scented floral garlands and presented with boxes of fireworks every year, my playroom festooned with scores of padeems – little clay Diwali lamps – that I begged from my indulgent hosts.

After all this initial exposure to so much ecumenical colour and light, however, moving to Pakistan was a little like travelling from the Vatican to a Scottish Free Kirk in the Hebrides, and it took a little time to learn to love the more subtle festivities of the Islamic faith. Mosques, with their slender minarets pointing joyous fingers up to God were always places of fascination, but their bushy-bearded imams were not particularly welcoming to curious white boys, and I was left to glean what I could about the Prophet from my Muslim friends after their weekly Diniyat lessons.

The country had just concluded the month-long fast of Ramadan, where participating Muslims partake of no food or water between sunrise and sunset each day.

Most of my friends were, thankfully, considered too young to actually fast themselves, and Mafzal had no intention of giving up his paan and cigarettes for something as trivial as the glory of God, but Alfie stoically observed the strictures, which must have been particularly gruelling for him when his duties included the serving of all our meals during what must have become very long days indeed.

However, the month of privation has finally drawn to its conclusion, and now, several weeks later, my young ally tells me with excitement in his eyes of the coming festival of Bakra Eid, where each family would buy an animal for ritual slaughter, dividing their sacrifice equally between themselves, their friends and the poor. Alfie is looking forward with anticipation, he says, to returning to his village for the first time since entering our employ and sitting at his parents' table for this ritual feast, and he regales me with tales of the fine cattle market that would soon come to the fallow paddy fields just beyond the mill's outer walls.

Going to school the next morning I ask Mafzal about this, and he nods, pointing out of the car window to show me a couple of small pens that have already been erected by early-bird traders, and, as the days pass and the festival draws nearer, more and more drovers appear with their livestock. I ask if it's permissible for me to go to see the market, and Mafzal says yes, but recommends we go at night, and, after assuring my parents that I will not be let out of their collective sight for a fraction of a nanosecond, he and Alfie take me down to the bustling fair.

Normally run-of-the-mill agricultural land, the local rice fields have tonight been transformed into a scene out of the Arabian nights, and under a canopy of twinkling stars a huge market lit by oil lamps and flaming torches spreads as far as the eye can see. There are cattle pens everywhere, packed with the best cows, sheep and goats available – as Islam prohibits the ritual slaughter of substandard beasts – and there are even strange curly-horned rams for religious purists who wish to sacrifice the same animal as the prophet Ibrahim.

Every family in the district is here in their best clothes, from the wealthiest landowners to the poorest farmers, with everyone buying the finest animals that they can afford, and, of course, every street vendor within a hundred-mile radius has also shown up to cash in on the trade, and there are food sellers of every description as well as a myriad of hurdy-gurdy men with monkeys and dancing bears. Music blares from fifty different radios and Victrolas, and Alfie, his eyes shining, points out the fine black and white goat that his father has put down a deposit on, and which he will personally lead back to his village in one day's time.

After the carnival atmosphere of the night market, the lustre on the Festival of Sacrifice tarnishes somewhat on the morning of Bakra Eid, when I suddenly become aware of packs of pariah dogs sniffing excitedly at pools of dried blood in front of people's homes, and during the day a steady procession of Muslim friends call at the house bearing sides of beef and legs of mutton.

We have been invited to the official Eid reception at the club, and we arrive there after dark to find the entire front lawn covered over with a titanic marquee constructed from bamboo poles and hessian, its inner ceiling lined with thousands of gleaming fairy lights, while huge illuminated oil drums fitted with fluttering strips of red and orange silk stand all along its tented back walls.

Traditional musicians are playing loudly amplified sitars and drums, and a barbecue kitchen has been built near the veranda, where twelve sweltering chefs are cooking enough spicy meats to feed the historical armies of Alexander for an entire campaign. The night air is redolent with the scents of garlic and wood smoke, and there are people ritually embracing everywhere, with normally conservative men now dressed in long satin coats with flashing jet buttons; their wives resplendent in their best silk saris and dripping in gold and rubies.

Vera and Cindy are ensconced at a nearby table with their husbands and friends, and, spotting us, they gesticulate enthusiastically and call us over to their enclave.

'Come over and have a seat,' Vera shouts over the din, as fleets of bearers ferry huge salvers of sizzling mutton tika over to the groaning boards at the centre of the marquee. 'There's no chance of getting any food yet. I've been up there twice but the buffet table's covered in small children just standing eating from the plates, no one else can get in until they've had their fill!'

'Come, come, Vera,' Dr Ahmed, Cindy's genial husband chides with a twinkle in his eye, 'suffer the little children. Is that not the proper Islamic way?'

'I think "suffer the wee wains" was Jesus, not Mohamed, dear,' Cindy, magnificent tonight in finely beaded emerald silk with a verdant corsage in her flaming red hair, says drily, and her portly husband laughs.

'As ever, I stand corrected by my pretty wife,' he says affectionately as a team of bearers arrive at our table with huge platters of barbecued meat and steaming freshly-baked naan breads. 'Hello, what is all this? Who has sent you fellows?'

'The Secretary Sahib, Doctor Sahib,' the burrah bearer replies, 'he was most concerned that Vera Memsahib has not been given enough food and has told us to bring plentiful supplies here to her very table so that she may not go hungry on this holy night.'

March has faded into a stark April and the mild winter weather is but a hazy memory of former days as a blistering-white sun scorches everything in its merciless path. The nights are hot and airless, and the daylight hours have already become unbearable by the time we have reached school in the morning, the car quickly transformed into an oven on wheels. Alfie's grey-bearded father arrives on the first of the month to collect his son's wages, and informs our faithful retainer that his wedding will be held in the village when the rains come, something that is news to us all, especially Alfie, who has not, as yet, met his betrothed.

Brother Pious uses the extreme temperature to punish the entire school for some misdemeanour that I can no longer remember, and we are all made to stand in line in the full sun for the entirety of our fifteen-minute morning recess, a chastisement so severe that it leads to several of the smaller boys fainting from the intense warmth. I spend any daylight hours not at school in the swimming pool, but even its sparkling blue waters are powerless to assuage the fierce heat of the pre-monsoon sun.

My dad orders the large mill doors to be removed from their hinges to try and create a through draft in the inferno that has replaced his jute factory, but even this measure can do nothing to calm the intense temperatures inside, and he comes home each evening looking like he has been put through a mangle backwards.

By six o'clock there is no breeze at all, and my parents and I take to sitting on a rickety wooden bench in our back garden once the sun has started to set each evening, trying desperately to catch a breath of air. The twilight sky is a dirty pink and purple, flecked by wildfire lightning which flickers away for hours and scents the air with a metallic sulphurous aroma, and we sit like cartoon imperialists listening to the BBC World Service on a tiny shortwave radio, the soft chiming of Big Ben the polar opposite of the crackling atmosphere all around us.

The dog has taken to spending his days sleeping with his tummy up hard against my parents' bedroom door to absorb what he can of their air-conditioned atmosphere, and it becomes an almost daily ritual for my dad to fall over him when he departs back to the mill after his afternoon siesta. However, come nightfall we cannot coax him into the house for all the bones in China – the dog, that is, not my dad – and he digs himself deep holes in the garden so that he can sleep with the coolness of the earth all around him.

As we slide into an even more punishing May, and frequent power failures leave the already fairly redundant fans completely useless, everyone abandons the house completely for the garden and veranda, and, in desperation one sleepless night we all pile into the car and my dad drives us through the darkness in hope of catching some hint of breeze by the simple act of motion.

As a ploy it works fairly well, and after driving for what seems like hours we stop at a small teashop in the middle of nowhere to buy cold Cokes and freshly-cooked spicy chicken, and we all sit out with our food on the embankment at the side of the road with the village folk. The darkness buys us anonymity, and we sit quietly watching groups of men sitting around their simple oil lamps on the hard-baked earth, playing cards or just sitting silently observing the brightly-coloured moths that hover around their sputtering naked flames.

'Rain,' everyone seems to whisper wherever we go, until the word becomes like a subconscious heartbeat. 'Rain. Rain. Rain. Why won't it rain?'

CHAPTER 11

the deluge

Art has never played a big part in our school curriculum, and the previous year's lessons have consisted of fifteen minutes on a Friday morning working from something called *The Pak Drawing Book*, a slender pamphlet printed on cartridge paper which features a very basic line drawing of a vase on one page with the opposite side purposefully blank, and all of us would-be Van Goghs are left to create our own sunflower compositions while our teacher catches up with his marking.

Brother Jean-Paul, however, a fervent painter himself, tolerates no such neglect of our creativity, and stretches the weekly 'drawing' time-slot into an hour to instruct us all in the techniques of the masters, illustrating his points with large copies of famous works of art in his own hand. A man on fire, he rejects the single pencil that is listed on our sheet of annual school requirements, and encourages us instead to go out to the new market and buy pastels and crayons, and even makes so bold as to teach us about abstraction, exhibiting the boldest of our daubs in the school assembly hall.

I find myself entranced by this earnest and passionate man and hang on to his every word, even to the extent of voluntarily coming back to school in the late afternoon to attend his extracurricular art classes, bribing Mafzal with paan and cigarettes to work round my mother's mah-jong

schedule to get me there and back without disruption to the rest of the household.

Thus I find myself in a ground-floor classroom overlooking the cemetery one sweltering afternoon in late May, laboriously attempting to capture a likeness of some wilted flowers baking on the cracked earth of a recent grave, when Brother holds his hand up for silence and cups the other to his ear.

'Listen, boys,' he says in a loud whisper, 'listen!'

But there is no need to listen because I can already smell it, that distinctive aroma of wet grass and flowers and earth, that much-longed-for scent of resurrection and rebirth in our parched and arid land.

Rain.

Rain falling softly onto the dry soil; rain suddenly slashing down into the scorched yellow grass; rain thudding onto the hot tin roof of the veranda with a rhythmic rat-a-tat-tat. Wet, saturating, drenching, rain.

The monsoon has begun.

Heedless of God's covenant to Noah the welcome rain pours down unceasingly, turning the cracked earth into rich loam and filling the irrigation channels in the barren paddy fields to bursting point. Rejoicing in its cool wetness I spend the entirety of the next afternoon in the garden dressed only in my swimming trunks, bounding in puddles like Gene Kelly and splashing my ecstatic dog with great torrents of muddy water as the two of us leap and jump through the downpour.

Two days later, the still pond that adjoins the mill boundary, previously a brown muddy puddle, bursts its banks and flows over into hollows on our side of the fence, and Alfie and I go out in the early morning armed with an impromptu fishing net and scoop up shoals of small brightly-coloured fish, like silver guppies, and fill the old aquarium on the back veranda with the glittering sprats.

The head mali, in trepidation of what is to come, calls in all available hands to bring in our considerable tomato crop, and my mother and myself, along with Mafzal and all the house servants, go out into the mud with the gardeners every break in the storm to harvest bucketfuls of the heavy red fruits. The fridge and storeroom are quickly filled, and tomato dishes abound at table, but even after everyone we can think of has been sent a huge box of the rich scarlet bounty, we are no nearer to clearing the glut of a crop that is still forming on the waterlogged plants.

Rumours of severe flooding are creeping in from the villages, and at Wallace's riverside mill the drowned body of a farmer is found washed up not far from the residential quarter, while our school is closed due to the inability of many boys to reach the building without being drenched by the deluge.

I'm sitting on the back veranda watching the day's downpour when I hear the internal phone's insistent ringing in the lounge, and am surprised to hear my dad's anxious voice on the other end of the line.

'Max, is the house flooded yet?' he demands, and I know that this is no joke because I can hear the panic in his voice. 'The main drain's blocked and the water's rising. Get Mafzal and that bloody fool bearer of yours and get up to the burrah maidan before we're all under water!'

He rings off before I have a chance to say, 'There's flooding and I'm getting to come and help?' and, yelling for Alfie, we quickly get hold of Mafzal and bundle into the car to drive the couple of hundred yards through the torrent up to the source of the drama.

The mill boasts a deep six-foot-wide storm drain which normally handles anything that the heavens choose to throw down, but today the foamy brown water laps just inches from the top, and, at the burrah maidan where we had all sat to watch the British Council film show not three months ago, there's a low concrete bridge where the swirling flood has burst the banks and is surging over the grass to lap hungrily at the steps of the under-managers' quarters.

My dad and the Captain are standing ankle-deep in water, yelling orders to drenched men with ropes, while women in wet saris are bundling possessions out of the ground-floor flats and storing them in the homes of their upper-floor neighbours.

Mafzal brings the car to a screeching halt in about four inches of water but notably doesn't leave the driving seat.

'Is it the damn water hyacinth, Sahib?' he yells over the noise of the storm and my father nods.

'Tell them to fix the rope onto the back of the car and I will pull it clear,' the driver yells, and Alfie and I pile out to assist a trembling mill worker who has volunteered to go into the swirling cauldron to attach the first line.

Heavy ropes are tied securely around the man's sinewy waist, and about twelve of us take the strain as he is lowered tentatively into the maelstrom. I am thoroughly enjoying myself in the midst of all this Moby Dick adventure, but I am suddenly jolted out of my complacency when the current grabs hold of the muscular body of the volunteer and yanks us all to the brink, and, even though more hands grab the rope, it is a struggle to keep him from being swept away and get him back to the safety of the bank.

Eventually, after what seems an age, he drops exhausted on the sodden grass, and men who normally secure the massive bales of hessian for transportation affix the line to the back of the car, which Mafzal, still warm and dry in his seat, puts tentatively into gear and starts to inch forward.

The rope goes taut but nothing budges, and the Vauxhall's engine begins to whine with the strain. 'I think we need to get the truck,' I hear the Captain yell to my dad over its banshee wail, but just as my father is about to nod ascent there's a rumble from under the bridge and a huge tree branch wrapped in water hyacinth emerges like the Loch Ness Monster, and the car shoots forward dragging it up on to the grass, while the flood waters immediately begin to subside.

Elsewhere the floods are not so easily dealt with, and our cook's village in the Karnaphuli valley near the hydro dam at Kapti is swept away when officials open a flood-gate to prevent the reservoir from bursting its banks, destroying many of the houses and farms in the path of the great torrent of water that they release.

As soon as we hear the news my mother packs the cook off onto a bus with twenty rupees to discover if he still has a home and family, and we get a message back the next day saying that all is well but that he has been bankrupted by a boatman who has taken everything he has in return for ferrying his loved ones to safety, and Mafzal and I immediately drive out to the muddy hill roads to pick him up.

We find him standing forlornly in a roadside shelter erected by soldiers, his house and animals gone and his wife and children left in what they stand up in. We obviously cannot leave the family stranded thus, and though I try to get a message back to my parents I end up taking the decision into my own hands, and, telling Mafzal that we'll take the entire family with us, pack wife, sister-in-law and miscellaneous babes into the Vauxhall and head for home.

Our normally very restrained cook is beside himself and clutches my hands in gratitude, babbling his thanks in English, Urdu and some third dialect that I don't recognise, but Mafzal tells him not to get his hopes too high until the Manager Sahib has given his blessing to the arrangements. However, seeing the anxious eyes of the frightened women and children in the back seat, I tell our cynical driver to keep his opinions to himself if he ever wants to mooch the price of another cigarette from me again, and I reassure the refugees that there is no question over them finding safe haven at our home.

News of our arrival has preceded us, however, and my mother has already arranged dry clothes and food for the family, while Alfie has vacated the servants' quarters and made temporary lodging for himself and the cook on the back veranda so that the ladies can have somewhere private to reside. My father makes an outward show of grumping about the inconvenience of having 'bloody hangers-on' in his house, but secretly gives the cook two hundred rupees to help rebuild his home and buy new goats when the waters subside, while the two women, used to field labour, quickly befriend the malis and set to work in the garden, swiftly bringing in the remainder of the tomato glut and then tilling the land for next season's maize.

It will take more than a simple act of God to disrupt my mother's mah-jong schedule, and play carries on regardless through the worst of the June downpours and into July without interruption. However, as the rains begin to abate and the cook's family go back to reclaim their homestead, a tremor runs through the world of ivory tiles when the quiet Betty, the fourth member of my mother's mah-jong foursome, announces that her husband's contract is about to expire and that they are retiring home to Scotland.

News of the empty seat travels like wildfire, and various ladies immediately begin to compete for the coveted place at my mother's table, with gifts of expensive silk and perfume suddenly appearing at the house in the company of soft-spoken servants who convey their mistress's compliments before departing.

The three witches – my mother, Vera and Cindy – get into huddle after huddle trying to choose a suitable successor, but to no avail, and eventually it is decided that a mah-jong party extraordinaire will be held in our house and that all the suitable candidates will be invited to take part in a kind of Mah-jong Super-Bowl to determine which one will be Betty's replacement.

Our bungalow is cleaned from top to bottom and a fleet of green baize gaming tables is borrowed from here, there and everywhere, and on the day of the big game the entire household is galvanised into action from six in the morning with the malis constructing massive floral displays while the cook prepares every kind of finger food known to man, yelling mercilessly at the unfortunate Alfie who has been drafted in to cut the crusts off sandwiches and prepare the salvers for the tables.

I'm on holiday from school and planning to hide in my room for the entirety of the tournament, but am button-holed by my mother en route to safety and placed on her meet and greet team as the parade of vehicles start to arrive, and, once all the grand memsahibs are seated, I'm seconded by the cook to help Alfie ensure that everyone's tea cups are kept filled and an endless supply of cold drinks travels from the fridge to the ice-buckets in the gaming room.

My mother is ensconced at the head table with Vera and Cindy, and winners from each of the other foursomes are dispatched to try their skill against them, but midway through the vetting process I'm waylaid by a corpulent middle-eastern woman called Nina, who pulls me to one side outside the cloakroom as I pass with an armful of empty Coke bottles.

'Max, darling, you haven't been to see me for so long,' she simpers, pinching my cheek and patting me affectionately. 'Is my new house not grand enough for you now?'

'New house, Aunty?' I say, perplexed. 'I didn't know you'd moved.'

'Moved?' Nina says, loudly, her freshly-rouged and powdered cheeks wobbling with emotion. 'Moved? We have not moved, my darling. We have been thrown out, after thirty years of loyal service they have kicked my Arthur into the gutter so that some jungly gunda can steal his job!'

'I'm sorry, I don't understand, Aunty Nina,' I say, hoping that I can soon escape back to the world of sanity. 'What's happened to Uncle?'

Nina rifles in her huge Mrs Khrushchev plastic handbag and hauls out a blurry photograph of a chubby-cheeked businessman cut from the local newspaper.

'This fellow,' she spits, 'this damn gunda has thrown my Arthur from his position and me from my lovely house because he wants your Uncle's job for one of his relatives. And what is the reason they are giving for dismissing my Arthur after thirty years of loyal service working his fingers to the bone? That he is a foreigner and I am a Jewess! I, a Jewess! Hah! I, who am the daughter of the best-known Baptist preacher in all of Lebanon, am a Jewess! I, who go to church every Sunday, am a Jewess! Pah! I spit upon them all!'

'Steady on now, Aunty,' I say anxiously, trying to keep her calm, but it is already too late as the rotund lady waves the offending photograph in the air and spits on it.

'Pah, see, there, I spit on you! See, I drop you in the dirt and stand on you! I even wipe my backside with you! Gunda! Peon! Buckas wallah!'

Where this tirade would have gone from here I don't know, but at this point my mother sticks her head around the cloakroom door and wants to know what's going on.

'Oh nothing you need worry about,' I say, 'but I think I've found your mah-jong fourth. Aunty here will fit right in with the rest of you.'

CHAPTER 12

CINEMA PARADISO

A huge luxury cinema called the Almas opens in the centre of Chittagong, and, well before multiplexes have made local Odeons redundant all over the length and breadth of Britain, announces that it will feature a second smaller auditorium within the building that will show only English-language movies.

The main hall is a true motion picture cathedral in the classic Grauman's style, with row upon row of plush velvet seats, a huge screen and forty-foot-high murals of dancing girls all along its softly illuminated walls, and no one in the town has seen its like before.

For the palace's maiden feature the proprietors secure a scratchy print of the Taylor-Burton *Cleopatra*, which they select to show off their giant screen, and all of Chittagong flocks to see this wonder of cinematic art, making tickets impossible to obtain for people like my family who have neglected to book in advance. After its initial three-week run, Elizabeth Taylor's sex and sand marathon is quickly replaced by the latest Bollywood hit, but the management is as good as its word and continues to feature daily foreign movies while it awaits the opening of its second auditorium.

My mother and I are in seventh heavens of delight over this new attraction, and we often travel straight from school to take in some weird piece of cinematic

psychodrama at the one-thirty matinee, grabbing samosas and mango juice from the foyer café, but my father remains unimpressed and wants to know why we can't be content with just watching films in the comfort of the club.

'The comfort of the club?' my mother says, looking at him askance. 'We all sit there on hard seats in the heat listening to all your bally mill hound friends snoring their way through the pictures, how is that comfortable?'

'Aye, well, we've had many a good night at the Anglo-India club pictures,' my dad mutters defensively, turning his back on us, 'and the club here's good enough for me...'

My earliest childhood memories of entertainment in India in the days before TV all feature going to the cinema, and Calcutta's town centre abounded with plush softly-aromatic picture palaces the like of which could not be bettered outside of Los Angeles. However, although my mother and I spent nearly all our spare time together in these air-conditioned halls of luxury, family cinema-going was more of a harum-scarum affair, and when my father was in tow we patronised not the grandiose movie cathedrals of Chowringhee but the rough and tumble halls of the numerous jute mill clubs instead.

Therefore, weekly 'Bioscope Nights' at Calcutta clubs like the ones my father so fondly remembers were more jute wallahs' social gatherings than experiences of big screen entertainment, and my dad's happy memories of good times at the Anglo India Jute Mill Club have very little to do with the quality of the films themselves. Despite its diminutive size this particular club boasted its own swimming pool, and movies were shown in the minute open-fronted club-house to the left of the water, the projectionist being positioned on a raised stand on the poolside patio outside so that he didn't expire from the heat of his machine.

Starting times were lax, being dependent on how quickly the sprawling audience could be herded up and shooed into the hall, and, as there was only one sixteen-millimetre projector, there were intervals every time the sweltering projectionist needed to change a reel, and the bar and sweetshop did a brisk trade each time the familiar white blobs appeared at the side of the rickety screen and the programme ground to an abrupt halt.

All the children would be bunched up the front of the auditorium in a noisy gaggle, while our parents skulked near the rear of the hall to get the benefit of the breeze that came in off the water, and we would rush over with hands outstretched for rupee notes for sweets and Coca-Cola every time the lights came up.

As the night wore on, however, the intervals would get longer and longer as the grown-ups lingered at the bar, and the children would raise a swelling chant of, 'Lights off, lights off!' until one of the club officials would eventually flick the switch and plunge the hall into the darkness, the film starting up to mutters of, 'Who's this in my seat?' as alcohol-fuddled jute wallahs fumbled their way through the dark.

Compared to my memories of India, the bioscope hall in the Chittagong club was the Empire in Leicester Square, but though the facilities here boasted a perm-anent screen and a proper booth with two projectors, the cinema experience at the club still leaned firmly towards the erratic. Films were never shown in one continuous ninety-minute run, it being considered essential to have an interval for food and drinks half-way through the performance, and though the bar bearers tried to make up orders in advance there was always a certain amount of confusion over who had whose whisky and soda, and people who had ordered food would tend to wander off in search of it, thus making the fifteen-minute intermission stretch to half an hour or more.

We also quickly discover that the monthly Gestetner-printed programme that the club management sends out is never to be trusted, and even if you are at the venue on the afternoon of a show the advertised event will not necessarily be the feature that you end up seeing that evening. At first we find this intensely frustrating, especially when we show up to see Danny Kaye in *The Secret Life of Walter Mitty* and are treated to Peter Cushing in *Dr Terror's House of Horrors* instead, which scares the living daylights out of me, so my dad takes to phoning the club before setting out to ascertain what is actually going to be on exhibition, but after a few months in the town we soon acclimatise and learn to take pot luck and watch whatever is on show that particular night.

The Almas, of course, is more predictable than the club and tends to show what it promises, without interruption. However, whichever auditorium you choose to patronise, there is nothing that quite prepares a British person for the eccentricity of foreign-language cinema in the subcontinent, and the choice of films on offer in our locality is alarmingly eclectic. It can only be assumed that the distributors in Chittagong pick their movies by one criteria alone, that being that the features have an English soundtrack, and the mixed bag of motion pictures that we see during our days of matinees at the Almas is quite hair-raising in its variety.

Italian art movies from the likes of Fellini cheerfully rub shoulders with Norman Wisdom comedies, while two-colour Technicolor Hollywood musicals and melodramas from the forties and fifties are equally staple fare. There is also a plethora of eccentrically-dubbed commercial thrillers from Japan and Hong Kong, and, of course, Italian sword and sandal epics from Cinecittà abound, not to mention Russian and Chinese communist treatises.

I've always assumed that the prints were bought second or third-hand from the west, and that when a film had well and truly had its day on the British or American grind house circuit it was packed into a crate and duly shipped off to East Pakistan. Scratches and snowstorms were everyday occurrences, and most movies had been suitably chewed at their reel ends, thereby making the action jump by anything from a few seconds to several minutes every time the projectionists performed a changeover.

Added to this was the fact that English-language features were being shown by technicians who often didn't speak the lingo, so if reels had been placed in the wrong cans by the previous cinema the story would be shown in lopsided order, and I can remember many an afternoon sitting in the Liberty Ice Cream Parlour trying to piece together the correct sequence of events of the show we had just witnessed. Even funnier was the occasion when we had all settled down to watch a scratchy print of the nineteen-forties Douglas Fairbanks horse-opera, *The Corsican Brothers*, when the projectionist had realised that he had inadvertently shown a reel from the end of the movie at the beginning, and had obligingly re-inserted it in its correct place so as not to disrupt his audience's enjoyment of the feature.

All of this was a fairly minor nuisance, however, when compared to the severity of the locality's draconian censorship laws, and although enfant terrible directors may have been challenging the old Hayes Board's social mores all over the globe, in East Pakistan men still kept their feet firmly on the floor at all times. Locally produced Bengali features were made with all the laws of the land in mind, of course, and the censors dealt with the sexual revolution in foreign films by simply removing any scenes they deemed offensive. Great chunks of plot or dialogue were frequently lost from some thriller or gladiatorial orgy scene because a buxom starlet crossed a room in her underwear.

tROUbLE at mill

A highly important component of the jute wallah's colonial lifestyle is the availability of a Brit-friendly Chinese restaurant, and the Tai Wah in Chittagong duly echoes to the dulcet tones of Dundee accents every Sunday night. The weekend 'Chinkie feast' is, of course, an unmissable mill hound ritual, and every jute town in the east has countless stories from its own oriental watering hole; my own particular favourites being the tales my mother would tell of her convent school days in Calcutta, when she and her sisters would sneak away from the nuns to enjoy illicit chow mein at a seedy establishment enticingly called the Hole in the Wall.

This forbidden eatery has long since gone when my memory of the bustling Indian city kicks in, and by then all the Calcutta jute wallahs were colonising a flashier establishment called the Waldorf, a large atmospherically-lit diner with huge frescos of China on its back wall and cut-out dragons with glowing red eyes adorning its many alcoves and arches.

By comparison to this fond memory, then, the Tai Wah is rather more austere, with its plain white-washed walls and obligatory moving waterfall picture on the wall, but the mill dogs have all rejected the more prestigious Peking Palace and the scruffier dockside Hong Kong Cafe, as run by my friend Arnold's dad, in its favour.

It must be said that there is something of a speakeasy air to the jute wallah's eatery of choice, however, the Tai Wah having no advertising sign and being reached by ascending a rather dark set of stairs in a dimly lit side street, a mere stone's throw from the city's red light district.

A small window in the door would open to your ring and a pair of heavily mascaraed eyes would survey you, then the door would be flung open and you would be welcomed like a long-lost relative by the beautiful Mrs Chang, the proprietress.

I often used to wonder why Mrs Chang didn't just get a copy of the nineteen sixty-five menu for the Calcutta Waldorf and have it duplicated, since none of the jute wallahs ever bothered to read her list of choices, asking instead for their favourite dishes from the old days, and leaving it to the Tai Wah's fleet of patient bearers to order up the equivalents from the smoky kitchen.

Even my highly conservative father, who after over three decades in the subcontinent has still not adapted to Indian food, is a hardened chop suey aficionado – much to the disgust of his fleet of Aunties back home – and seven o'clock sharp every Sunday night sees us all at our usual table at the Tai Wah, conversing with the imported-silk-clad Mrs Chang and making short work of salvers of butterfly prawns and bowls of noodles.

On this particular Sunday a party of French interlopers has crashed the restaurant, and the Dundee crowd have been excelling themselves with sweet-and-sour-frogs-legs jokes, blissfully unaware of what's being flung back at them *en Français*. Mrs Chang, looking like a rotund Anna May Wong in a tight, intricately-embroidered silk cheongsam, walks the aisles between the two sets of tables like a school prefect on dinner duty, chatting and smiling amiably while she makes sure no one progresses to blows in the impromptu territory-marking war, when the night's genial ambience is suddenly shattered by an insistent pounding on the stair-head door.

Mrs C slides back the viewing panel and then quickly opens the door, and a breathless Cindy and Doctor Ahmed barge into the room, which has suddenly gone very quiet indeed.

Cindy's face is ashen, and even the unflappable Doctor looks visibly shaken as the two of them flop down at the nearest table, Cindy's hand clutching at her chest as she attempts to speak.

'Missy Cindy, Missy Cindy, what is wrong?' Mrs Chang demands anxiously, motioning to her burrah bearer to bring glasses of water. 'Has someone tried to rob you?'

'Worse,' Cindy replies breathlessly, 'something's happened, they've declared hartal...'

There's a moment's pin-drop silence in the busy room, broken only by a puzzled French voice asking 'Qu'est-ce que c'est l'hartal?' Then everybody begins speaking at once.

'Are we stuck? Have they barricaded the roads?' I hear someone ask above the general uproar, and then Vera's voice cuts through the hubbub wailing, 'Are they burning cars? Oh my God, they're burning cars, aren't they? I told you not to bring the Merc!'

'Everyone, quiet please,' Mrs Chang commands, holding her hands up for silence. 'I have a very fine portable radio from Taiwan in the kitchen, we will all find out what is happening presently. Missy Cindy, drink some water, and everyone else, your food is getting cold. We are all safe here.'

She vanishes through the swing doors into the kitchen with a swish of satin, and Vera and her husband grab their plates and dash over to our table as soon as she has passed from view.

'This has been brewing for months,' Vera whispers confidentially, compulsively stuffing battered shrimp into her mouth. 'The Awami League keep protesting about the situation and the government's doing nothing...'

'Damn rabble,' Cindy breathes, also seating herself at our table, 'the government needs to flog the lot of them!'

'But what's wrong?' I ask, and all the adults turn to me as one.

'Oh, we're frightening the boy,' Vera fusses. 'It's all right, chicken, we're all safe here...'

'I know that,' I say patiently, secretly quite looking forward to the possibility of having to camp out in the restaurant overnight. 'I want to know why the people are so angry?'

There's a momentary pause, then Doctor Ahmed explains, 'The government is far away in West Pakistan, Max, and the folks here feel that they're being ignored by the people who are taking all their taxes, and something has happened tonight that's made them all very angry, so they're barricading the roads to stop the town from working properly so that the government will have to take notice of them...'

'But it's Sunday,' I say, genuinely perplexed. 'No one's working tonight. Why have a general strike now?'

'Because the damned rabble never did have a good sense of timing,' Vera interjects grumpily.

The incident of that Sunday night is soon dealt with and life quickly returns to normal, but although the flame has been extinguished, the fuse on this particular powder keg is still smouldering and it would erupt spectacularly in the war of independence in 1971.

We all go back to work and school, but a sense of general unease grips the whole town, and the white community watches powerless as Muslim slowly turns against Muslim in the run-up to the approaching civil war. As the year progresses and Christmas comes and goes, there are more and more protest rallies and strike days, and 'hartal' soon becomes the in-word on everyone's lips.

In our first summer in the town, Ayub Khan, the president of Pakistan, had visited as part of his national goodwill tour, and every factory and mill had lined his route with intricate floral arches of welcome; hundreds of us standing out in a drenching monsoon downpour to watch his motorcade drive slowly by. Now, a scant fifteen months later, demonstrators regularly burn his effigy in public, and signboards in English and Urdu are stoned and pelted with cow dung as the cry of 'Bengal for Bengalis' is heard throughout the land.

Things come to a head, unsurprisingly, in the hot months of early nineteen sixty-nine, and general strikes are being held almost daily as disgruntled workers take to the streets to air their dissatisfaction with a government that cowers in its den over a thousand miles away. Tempers are running high in the blistering sun, and as we are sitting sweltering at our desks conjugating verbs one morning, our new teacher for nineteen sixty-nine, Sir Ivor, holds his hand up for silence and leans out of the unglazed window, one hand cupped to his ear.

We all strain to hear what is upsetting him, then, far down in the street, we hear it, the distant sound of a Tannoy on the back of a truck, where an agitated voice is declaiming passionately in rapid Bengali that I cannot quite make out, but one oft-repeated word is unmistakably clear.

Hartal.

Sir Ivor, who lives only a stone's throw away, hastily sends a boy to his house to collect a wireless set, and we tune into the local station, all of us crowded around the tiny transistor radio on our teacher's desk as we listen with horror to what has come to pass.

A politician called Sergeant Zahurul Haq, a beloved local figure and dedicated spokesman for East Pakistan in the popular Awami League, has been under arrest and awaiting trial, but today has been murdered in cold blood in his cell in Dacca by a West Pakistani constable, and riots have erupted throughout the city.

We all sit open-mouthed at the enormity of what has happened, things like murder and assassination being well beyond our ken, and, lessons forgotten, we are all sitting anxiously awaiting the next bulletin, when our headmaster, a short bald-headed French-Canadian monk, bustles breathlessly into our classroom.

'Boys, boys, my dear boys,' Brother says, clearly shaken, 'this is a terrible thing that has happened and we shall all pray for the family of this brave and most beloved man, but for now I am here to tell you that school is closed until further notice and that a procession is on its way here, and that they are seeking to collect every boy from our school and take them with them on their march. I cannot stop you from joining this protest, boys, but I would beseech you all not to march today as the army is on the streets with guns, and I would not like to be delivering the eulogy at the funeral of any boy from my school. So please, gather your books and go quietly home now while you still have time. God bless you, boys.'

It would be nice to say that we all filed out of the room in orderly fashion, but in actuality our exit is more like a painting of lost souls fleeing from Bedlam by Richard Dadd. Thundering down the stairs to the playground, we find our campus split into two, with two-thirds of the school heading for home while most of the older boys congregate at the open main gates in an angry chanting cluster.

I'm standing in the midst of all this turmoil, completely out of my depth and quite unsure of what I should do next, when a hand grips my elbow and propels me towards the side exit.

'Come on, man, we got to get home, quick,' Arnold's voice yells in my ear. 'You got any money so we can get a baby taxi? We can go to my house and you can phone your pop from there!'

'Can't we just phone from here?' I ask as I'm dragged across the playground. 'I'll get Mafzal to fetch us and you can come out to our place!'

Arnold laughs without humour. 'There's no phone to make the call, man. Brother's barricaded the office up in case they try to crack open the safe. Anyway, your driver won't be able to get here in time before they block all the roads. Come on, we got to go, now!'

We're on the main road, desperately trying to flag down a baby taxi in the crowds of fleeing boys and bullock cart drivers hastily getting their wares off the street before the protest marchers and any potential looters reach our quarter. The local shops, normally friendly places open from dawn till dusk, are all shuttered and dark, and the hot morning air echoes to the sound of blaring radios and angry voices, a discordant symphony regularly punctuated by the staccato hammering of merchants boarding their shops.

It's nearly noon and the bright-white sun is merciless, and, in desperation, Arnold steps out into the path of a speeding scooter-rickshaw driver and brings the tiny taxi to a screeching halt.

'What are you crazy bastards doing?!' the driver yells in Bengali, as Arnold whispers, 'Get in and don't budge whatever he says,' and we both pile into the back of the hot vehicle and sit tight.

'Take us down to the docks, man,' Arnold pleads. 'There's no trouble there.'

'No, no, no,' the driver counters, 'this is hartal, if they see me with two foreigners in tow they will burn my taxi and then who will feed my wife and many babies?'

'Taxi wallah, we are wasting precious time,' Arnold beseeches, adding, 'take out your money but don't hand it over,' sotto voce to me in English.

'I am just a poor and humble man,' the driver continues, closely counting up the rupee notes and change in my hand, 'I would need at least... double fare for such a risk to my livelihood!'

'But we have only enough for one and half, taxi wallah,' Arnold counters, but the driver remains firm.

'No, no, chotta sahibs, I need at least double or you must get out of my cab now!'

We can hear the livid chanting of the marchers by now as the huge procession moves slowly up the main road in the centre of town, and plumes of black smoke from burnt-out vehicles pierce the burning sky, telling Arnold that there is no more time to argue this particular round.

'Very well, taxi wallah, we will pay you double fare, but only if you drive now!' Arnold yells in Bengali, and the man obligingly revs the throttle on his handlebars and takes off in a cloud of dust, well satisfied with the deal he has just brokered.

Arnold flops back on the hot plastic seat and wipes his perspiring brow, whispering to me in English, 'Murgia, man, I thought that gunda was going to take us for triple money at least!'

We can clearly see the approaching mob as the little taxi roars off down the now almost deserted road of shuttered shops, a huge wall of surging humanity flowing down the canyon of the street like an angry river in full spate. Its leaders all carry sombre banners of black mourners' crêpe, completely bereft of any demand or slogan, and the noise of their angry voices is quite deafening as they pitch down the street, their fluttering ebony flags filling the air like heraldic standards at a medieval battle-field.

Hundreds of our senior pupils flock to join the already huge crowd, and our driver swears vociferously as he screeches past two blocked side streets, eventually finding a road that has not been barricaded with overturned vehicles, and we fly up it to the sound of stones and bottles bouncing off the taxi's flimsy roof.

'Oh my lord god, Allah, peace be upon him,' the driver wails, keeping the taxi at full throttle as we swerve past obstacles and angry protestors screaming at us to observe the hartal, 'why oh why did I take you damn fellows into my cab, now they will surely burn my taxi and hang me in the street for the pariah dogs to eat...'

'Just drive, taxi wallah,' Arnold yells into his ear above the din. 'There will be plenty of time for complaint later. Quickly! Go down that street there, we are getting out of their orbit now. See, there is clear road ahead and we are still alive!'

The driver swears unintelligibly as his taxi shoots forward like a rocket, scrapes past an upturned cart by inches and flies down the deserted road my friend has indicated, then onwards towards the docks and the safety of the Hong Kong Café.

I spend the rest of the day at Arnold's small house, eating noodles and jasmine tea with his grandmother and many little sisters, the restaurant downstairs shuttered against possible looters while we listen to the news bulletins on a rickety old wireless set that sits propped up on a carved-wood table by a statue of the Virgin Mary.

I phone home and get my dad about to leave for the strike-bound mill, who tells me to sit tight until the protest is over, and we sit listening to the reports of street clashes and mobs burning down government buildings until late into the evening. Grandma Pang starts to make up a bed for me at eight o'clock, fearing that the violence will not abate until the small hours, but my mother calls to say Mafzal has deemed it safe to come out, and the dark blue Vauxhall pulls into the restaurant's forecourt an hour later.

Thanking the Pangs effusively I slip out to the car, where I find my mother ensconced in the back seat like the Queen Mother, and Mafzal flashes me a look of long suffering, whispering, 'I could not persuade her to stay at home and the Manager Sahib was still at the mill calming the workers. Come, Chotta Sahib, sit in the front seat beside me and stay low down.'

Because of the extreme heat we normally drive with all the windows open, even after dark, but tonight Mafzal has wound every one tightly to the top and pushed the locks down on all his doors. The car has two fluttering black silk flags affixed to its front radiator grill, as have most of the vehicles that have ventured out into the streets, and we drive cautiously homewards like a hearse, staying clear of the main thoroughfares where armed soldiers are believed to be shooting at anything that moves.

We creep successfully through the shuttered town and over the railway lines at the deserted level crossing, and are just about to join the road that will take us out to the safety of the rice fields and home when we come head to head with a huge mob of protestors, black standards flying in the night breeze like monochrome caricatures of old Soviet propaganda posters.

There is nowhere to turn to get out of their path, and I can hear Mafzal, not known for his religious convictions, begin to mutter a silent prayer. The marchers' voices are low and surly, and many carry lanterns or flaming torches, and they advance steadily upon us like the tide, slowly and deliberately, their expressions unreadable in the dusky evening light.

'Keep driving, very slowly, Mafzal,' my mother's voice whispers from the back seat, 'and, Max, stay very low in your seat and let me do any talking that needs to be done...'

The huge crowd is upon us now, blotting out what little sunset light there is left, but, as Mafzal inches slowly forward, they part like the ocean to let us by, and I see my mother in the back seat gently waving like passing royalty at a funeral, meeting the eyes of the protestors with sympathy and commiseration for their loss, and we drive slowly through their midst to their murmured blessings of 'Peace be upon you, Auntie'.

CHAPTER 14

the shakespeare wallahs

We have all been barricaded in the house for the last four days, the mill shut down and becalmed as hartal rages in the streets and overturned buses smoulder where they have been left to halt the way of West Pakistani soldiers.

My father paces our quiet rooms like a caged animal, anxiously fretting about his mill and the fate of his many junior assistants who are billeted in the village beyond the safety of our high factory walls, while my mother sits silently playing endless games of solitaire, her head tilted to one side as she keeps an ear open for the sounds of trouble in the street outside.

On the fifth day the radio announces that the president has resigned and that the country is now under martial law led by General Yahya Khan, and, unhampered by restrictions on their power, his army sets about restoring order.

Gruff moustachioed men with scrambled egg all over their shoulders come to the house to see my father two days later, and they all go off to the mill together in an army jeep, the familiar heartbeat-sound of the machines resuming soon after, and a proclamation arrives in the mail announcing that all schools are to reopen on Monday.

It seems that the violence of the last few months is being swept systematically under the carpet, and, with the streets cleared of debris, the cinemas and shops reopen

and we are all told to get back to whatever semblance of normality we can aspire to. But although we're doing all the same things again, life is still very far from normal, and it's as if everything has subtly shifted, or perhaps it's just that I've grown up a little over the last few anxious days.

Certainly, I'm suddenly seeing life from a new perspective, and I'm sitting alone in the lounge on the Saturday before I'm due to go back to school, my nose, as usual, buried in a book, when the phone rings and I recognise my mother's friend Cindy on the other end of the line.

'Memsahib hai?' Cindy queries in very stilted Urdu, mistaking me for Alfie, but instead of just identifying myself as I would normally have done, I am suddenly seized by some unrecognised force and answer her back in the local dialect in the guise of our aspiring butler.

'Yes, Cindy Memsahib,' I say mischievously, 'but she is unable to come to the phone just now, for the Manager Sahib is at the mill and the Memsahib is making exceedingly good use of the time in the bedroom with some strange fellow…'

There's a boy who's been put into my class at school this year called Mohamed Farooqui, better known as Flick, who I've seen lounging around at the club swimming pool but never spoken to, but he stops beside me in the queue for the library on our first week back at school and drops his lunch box at my feet.

'Hey, man,' he says laconically, 'there's a drama on at the Chittagong Club next week. I've seen the pictures outside and it looks to be good. At least, they're hanging one fellow, so it can't be all bad. You want to go? Good, I'll pick you up at your place at seven o'clock.'

'But you don't know where I live,' I call to his back, but he simply makes a dismissive wave and disappears.

I have assumed that Flick has been pulling my leg and have forgotten all about our proposed man-date to view a celebration of the works of Eugene O'Neill – as sponsored by the US Consulate – when Alfie sticks his head around my room door the following Friday evening.

'Hello, Chotta Sahib,' he grins, 'one boy is calling you.'

'Who?' I say, perplexed, as Flick pushes Alfie to one side and strides into my room, looking all about him like a tourist inspecting ancient ruins.

'Hey, man, you got thousands of books! Were you thinking of going out like that? I think you need to put a tie on at least. Come on, I've squared it with your pop, hurry up and get ready!'

'You mean we're really going to see a play?' I ask, hastily pulling on a long-sleeved shirt, still reeling from the shock of hearing that my parents have sanctioned this unsupervised outing. 'I don't think I've ever been to anything like that before.'

'Some Shakespeare wallahs came to the school once, before you came, they were plenty terrible, man, but there was a girl in a short dress, so I stayed awake for that. This is American stuff tonight, though, so there's got to be some babes, no? Yes, that tie will do, come on, chalo, let us go!'

We fly through the lounge, Flick pausing just long enough to fling a casual 'Good night, Aunty!' to my mother and shake my dad's hand at the door, promising to have us back as soon as the show finishes.

'You boys behave, now,' my dad cautions as we leave, slipping me five rupees as I go out of the French windows, shell-shocked, and follow Flick to a bright red Triumph Herald that sits idling in the drive.

'Where's your driver, Flick?' I ask as I slide into the passenger seat, and my companion gives me a puzzled look.

'Driver? I don't need a driver, man,' he says, climbing in behind the wheel and putting the Triumph into gear. 'This is my car!'

'But, but, you're thirteen,' I say, flabbergasted, as we speed up the driveway and out through the mill gates. 'Are you allowed to drive?'

'If your old man's rich in this town you can do anything, man,' Flick replies as we fly up the dark road through the fallow rice fields. 'It was only a fifty-rupee bribe for the licence. You want one? My pop will fix it for you.'

I buy Mafzal a double helping of paan as we return home from school the next day and he looks at me suspiciously.

'Your amah has said that we are to be home promptly today, Chotta Sahib,' he says guardedly, 'I cannot take you anywhere off our route as there is mah-jong this afternoon, and nothing must interfere with that.'

'Oh, that's OK,' I reply casually. 'I didn't have anywhere I wanted to go…'

A knowing smile creeps over our driver's chubby face.

'Ah, you went to the club with Flick Sahib last night, Chotta Sahib,' he smiles, 'and now you want me to teach you how to drive.'

'Gosh, what a good idea,' I say innocently.

As I predicted, my mother's mah-jong coven have selected the eccentric Nina as their fourth member, and they are all well ensconced when I come in from school, their side tables littered with lipstick-stained cigarette butts and left-over sandwiches.

'Hello, my darling,' Nina smiles as I neatly sidestep her sloppy embrace. 'How is my chotta sahib today?'

'Oh, I'm fine, Aunty,' I reply, putting my school bag away. 'How's Uncle's court case going?'

'Oh slow, my darling, dangerously slow. They are all dragging their feet in the hope that we will be dead before they hear it. Damn Jungle-Jims that they are. Did I show you the picture of the fellow who's responsible for throwing my Arthur onto the street? I have wiped my backside with that fellow's face many times, I can tell you…'

'Yes, yes, we know,' Vera interrupts while Cindy pouts over her tiles, still sulking with me over my telephone charade of the previous week. 'Max, sweetheart, be a love and get me another Coke, we've rung and rung for your bearer but there's no sign of him.'

'Sure, Aunty,' I grin, knowing exactly where Alfie and the cook will be, it being a favourite ploy of theirs to retreat to their quarters after lunch so they can be conveniently out of earshot of the living room servant's bell; and I'm on my way to get Vera's drink myself when the phone rings.

'You still friends with that little fat bugger?' Flick's voice enquires.

'Arnold? Yes. Why?'

'Get your homework done now, man. We're going to his restaurant tonight.'

'But the food's not any good,' I reply, puzzled.

'We're not going to eat, man,' Flick says with a laugh.

We arrive at the Hong Kong Café a little after eight and find Arnold sitting at one of the empty tables with his school books, his fingers ink-stained as he labours over tonight's series of arithmetical problems.

'Murgia, boys,' he says in greeting, 'these sums are making my damn head spin. What you boys doing here so late, anyway?'

'Oh we've just come to see you,' Flick says innocently and Arnold raises a quizzical eyebrow.

'This fellow has maybe come to see me,' he says shortly, addressing Flick directly, 'but you're here to see my pop. Abah! Some business for you!'

There's a click-clack of beads as the strip curtain that divides the café from the Pang's living quarters parts slowly, and there stands Arnold's father, a slightly taller replica of my loyal school friend, dressed in brightly-coloured shorts and a silk bush shirt that could outdo a neon sign.

'Greetings, greetings, boys,' Mr Pang smiles. 'Come in, please, you are most welcome. You like my shirt? It was delivered from Hong Kong only yesterday, maybe I can find another for you, no?'

'No thank you, Uncle,' Flick says, turning on his charm, 'but perhaps you can find us some music?'

'Ah, music, yes,' Mr Pang muses, 'music is the food of love and something that might be obtained for the right sum of money. Arnold, bring some cold 7-Up for your guests. What did you want to hear, boys? Personally I like American jazz, you have preferences?'

'Ah, maybe American, Uncle, but UK is so-oo good just now,' Flick replies as Arnold brings two ice-cold bottles with straws bobbing in them. 'I would love to hear something by the Rolling Stones, if I could lay hands on such an item.'

'The Rolling Stones? Ah, very fine musicians indeed and much sought after, but such luxury items require high financial sacrifice. Would a boy like you be able to bear such deprivation?' Mr Pang counters, and Arnold, who has sat down to join us, whispers in my ear, 'You got any idea what's going on here, man?'

I shake my head bewilderedly and my friend laughs. 'You never wondered how my pop makes this place pay? Come on, man, no one ever comes here for the food.'

However, further dialogue is halted by Flick and Mr Pang reaching some sort of agreement, and a substantial pile of rupee notes surreptitiously changes hands under the table.

'Please to excuse me, boys,' Mr Pang says, giving a little bow, as he vanishes behind his curtain like the Wizard of Oz with an ominous rattle of beads.

'How much have you just paid him, Flick? And for what?' I ask, sounding like someone's horrified maiden aunt.

'Hey, relax, man,' Flick reassures me. 'It was only seventy bucks.'

'Seventy rupees? Why, that's more than Alfie earns in a month. What are you buying for that? Oh no, please tell me it's not a woman!'

Arnold and Flick fall about helplessly laughing at my naivety, and Mr Pang looks at them perplexedly as he returns to the table with a slim package.

'Ah, you are sharing some merry schoolfellow joke while I am out of the room, huh, boys?' he says good-naturedly. 'So, here is your gramophone record, Flick Sahib, *Let It Bleed* by the Rolling Stones brand new from Hong Kong this morning. You want more, you tell me soon, OK. There may another shipment next week where many wondrous things may be had. But remember, boys, discretion is the better part of valour!'

Mah-jong is being held at Nina's house today and Mafzal drops me there after school to wait for my mother, but the game is in full swing when I arrive, with piles of crumpled rupee notes amidst the tiles, and I'm heading for one of the battered old cane-weave armchairs in Nina's lounge to wait it out when the good lady calls me to her side.

'Hello, darling, we will be some while yet,' she coos, pinching my cheek. 'Tell the bearer to make you up a plate and then go up and see Uncle, he's on the roof.'

'On the roof, Aunty?' I say, surprised.

'Oh yes, darling, that is where he hangs out these days, whatever the weather. When he dies I'll just set fire to his desiccated corpse and he can burn away to glory all by himself up there.'

Visualising Arthur clinging tenaciously to the chimney pots, I hastily take my plate of cucumber sandwiches, climb the narrow stairway that the servant indicates, and open a coarse plank door to another world.

Arthur's flat rooftop has been transformed into a lush tropical garden that runs the length of the building within the parameters of an old chipped terracotta balustrade, every inch of space being covered in luxuriant plants and trees, with rows of vegetables in old ghee tins, fruit bushes in battered kerosene cans and young saplings in crudely-painted oil drums.

Arthur, a tubby old English burrah sahib with a droopy white walrus moustache, is busily tending to some tomato plants that are sagging with the weight of their rich plum-shaped fruit. He is dressed simply in white cotton trousers and a pale cotton shirt that has once been coloured but has turned pallid from frequent dhobi bleachings, wet stains showing under the armpits from where he has been labouring in the heat with his horticulture. He wears a large straw hat on his head which is fairly powerless against the punishing afternoon sun, but the leathery old Englishman seems oblivious to the possibility of discomfort and hails me cheerily as I walk across the hot concrete towards him.

'Hello there, young Max,' he calls in a strong old-school English accent, 'welcome to my little garden!'

'Wow, this is terrific, Uncle!' I exclaim, using Flick's current in-word of the week. 'When did you build all this?'

'Oh, over the last thirty years,' he chuckles without much humour. 'This is my garden from our old house.'

'From the old house...?' I say, realisation beginning to dawn.

'Yes, they can throw me out of my job and steal my home, damn them, but they can't have the fruits of my labour. When they said I had to go I dug up every tree and bush that I had ever planted and brought them here, one by one. I'm telling you, I've left a field like Passchendaele for their new man to try his hand with. Come on, since you're here you can help me water the tomatoes, they're thirsty little beggars now that they're living in old tin cans.'

going down to yasgur's farm

As the worst of the summer heat rages I fall victim to a malarial fever and pass the next three weeks deliriously tossing and turning in my bed, convinced that Wallace has visited me each day bringing the moon in a jar to light my sick-bed at nights. The suddenly grave mill doctor keeps me under semi-quarantine conditions, permitting only my mother and himself to enter my room, and when my fever finally breaks on the first day of the rains there is a collective sigh of relief from the entire household.

The doctor has barely walked out of my door when Alfie rushes in to see me, with Mafzal following as soon as he has returned the medic to his dispensary, grinning that he has missed my regular contributions to his paan and cigarette fund; and even my dad does an unheard-of thing and returns home from work early to sit by my side, muttering gruffly about what a bloody nuisance I've been.

It's another four weeks until I'm fit enough to return to school, but Arnold and Flick come out to visit me most afternoons, Flick bringing something called a compact cassette recorder – which is, apparently, all the rage in Karachi – and we sit watching the pouring rain and listening to ropy recordings of Herman's Hermits and Nancy Sinatra, easily kept to a volume that won't disturb my father's afternoon siesta hour.

'You really need to get yourself a record player, man,' Flick complains, looking about him at my shelves, 'instead of all these damn books. Fat Bugger, can your pop get him one from Hong Kong?'

'Too bulky, man,' Arnold replies, shaking his head, 'the shippy fellows won't risk bringing anything that size past customs.'

'Then we'll need to find you one,' Flick muses. 'Which burrah sahibs are leaving this month?'

Everyone has gone to the swimming pool on the Sunday before I am due to officially resume my studies, but I have missed so many films during my illness and convalescence that I cry off and go to the morning matinee at the Almas instead, determined to catch up on a re-run of a popular feature that has passed me by.

The big cinema is packed, but I manage to get a seat at the far back of the grand circle, an eyrie tucked away at the rear of the vast auditorium, perched perilously at the summit of several rows of steeply raked seating. I'm sitting waiting for the film to start with my nose buried in *The Coral Island* by R M Ballantyne, a Victorian adventure novel that has had me on the edge of my seat all of the previous night, when a young man in his early twenties seated next to me nudges me with his elbow.

'Would you look at those crazy foreigners, man,' he says with bitter amusement. 'These fellows have not realised that British rule is long since dead and buried.'

I look over in the direction of his gaze, and realise with horror that the objects of his ridicule are Wallace and his family, lording it up the centre aisle to the private boxes at the cinema's rear in stately procession. In fact, if Norman Rockwell had ever painted 'Members of the British Raj View the Cinematograph,' the tableau before me would mirror his composition brushstroke for brushstroke, and I sink fearfully down into my seat least my fellow countrymen should spot me and summon me into their presence.

Wallace leads the imperialist parade, striding amidst the rabble with his head held high like a British monarch heading for the royal box at some Empire gala, with Peggy, his dutiful consort, the requisite three paces behind him, the twins and their entourage in her wake, and Mary Magdolina, the little nunlike creature I had met earlier, bringing up the rear and looking as if she should be holding a parasol for her betters.

'Look, they are all heading for the ladies' boxes where only the purdah women go,' my companion whispers. 'They do not seem to have grasped that it is all share and share alike now. In fact, it would not surprise me if this fellow does not even have a car and has come here on his elephant instead. Promise me that you will relinquish all these ancient ways, my friend.'

Surprisingly, my parents do not raise too many objections to buying a record player, and, since I was in the grips of the fever on my thirteenth birthday, my dad agrees that such an item can indeed be purchased if we can find an available machine so far from western civilisation.

We take a walk around the new market but there's nothing doing in any of the many electrical shops, although an enterprising young clerk tries his hardest to interest us in a Japanese shortwave radio that will give us access to 'all the young people's music from around the globe,' so, with a list of all the about-to-be-departed in our hand, courtesy of Flick, we start out on a series of systematic visits to see what can be salvaged.

After two dead ends we strike gold at the third home we call at, and a frosty-faced English memsahib admits that, yes, they have a record player that they won't be taking with them when they depart, and, after a moment's hesitation, invites us into her home.

The house in question is a neat bungalow in a walled estate belonging to an old-school English shipping company, and all their neat Art Nouveau staff cottages sit nestled in the shade of a grove of leafy banyan trees, the sun dappling attractively on their long verandas. Unlike most of the people that my parents know, the English contingent here are all very much in the traditional mould, and my father and I are led grudgingly into an old colonial living room whose brown wood-stained décor is pure unadulterated E M Forster India.

'Well, this is it,' our host says stiffly, pointing to an ancient nineteen-fifties radiogram in a dark tan mahogany. 'It was a wedding present and has many sentimental memories for me, but we just can't ship everything back to Basildon when we go.'

My dad and I exchange a look and, when I nod hesitantly, Dad asks the lady to name her price.

'Oh, a price, well I'm not sure...' she stalls. 'It came from the best store in Dacca when my mother-in-law bought it for us, you know, and I'm sure it's still an item of considerable value.'

'Well, could you maybe give us hint of what you think that value might be?' my dad asks in his most tactful of voices, and the lady gives a little shudder of distaste before replying.

'Well, I thought, perhaps, because my mother-in-law did insist on getting us a genuine Morphy Richards machine, and, of course, all the valves still work, that I could maybe let it go... as a special favour... for... three hundred rupees.'

We both start visibly at the extremity of her price, and although I manage to bite my tongue, my dad, not known for his subtlety, exclaims, 'My god, are you throwing your mother-in-law in with that, woman?' and things go pretty much onto a downhill slope from there.

The lady says frostily that, no, she doesn't think that one hundred rupees would be a reasonable offer for something so sentimentally important, and, after my dad replies that he wouldn't be buying the sentiment and that she would be quite welcome to keep that for herself, an elderly bearer shows us quickly to the door, doing his very best to conceal an amused smirk.

No one else on the list appears to have anything to sell, and we are about to call it a day when we notice that there is one more name left, an Austrian banker and his wife known as Herr Freddie and Frau Hilda, and, not really expecting any result, we drive over to their spacious flat at the far end of town before heading for home.

Frau Hilda answers our ring herself and ushers us into a surprisingly attractive living room, the walls whitewashed in a cool shade of eau-de-Nil with a single vase of lush blooms on a low-slung coffee table, the entire place looking more like something out of an American magazine rather than the typical Chittagong apartment with its obligatory raffia furniture and turmeric-yellow walls.

There's also a grand piano with stacks of music on the lid, and Hilda seats herself at the stool as she smiles warmly in greeting at us.

'It is so nice of you to come and see me like this,' she says in strongly accented English. 'Freddie is out at the bank and will not be back until later, so I just sit here all afternoon and I play with myself.'

I just about manage to suppress a snort and my dad finds the need to cough violently, but the good lady continues oblivious, 'Yes, when my Freddie is here he can play a duet with me, and that is most good, but mainly it is just me, myself, so your visit is very welcome.'

A servant brings glasses of iced Benz, a locally-produced mango drink, as Hilda lets her fingers trail lazily over the keys.

'I so adore Mozart,' she sighs. 'Do you like symphonic music, Chic?'

'Oh yes, I'm a regular Mantovani man,' my dad mutters. 'We were wondering, Hilda, do you maybe have a record player that you want to sell, for my boy here?'

'Ah, the boy likes music? Yes, yes, there is an old one of Freddie's that we will not be shipping back to Vienna. Come, I will show it to you!'

We eagerly follow her more than ample form into the next room, where a hefty wooden box like a truncated coffin sits connected to a large valve radio, but Hilda lifts the lid to reveal a rather modern turntable within.

'We ordered this from Berlin and it came as just a deck, but my Freddie, he likes to carve wood in his spare time, so he made this box for it himself. We use this old radio to play it, but it has a nice sound. See, I show you.'

She flicks through a large pile of records and selects one, flipping it onto the turntable as the old wireless hums into life.

'Ah, now this, this is superb,' she says, as what I would later immediately recognise as the Queen of the Night's aria from *The Magic Flute* fills the room. 'Ah, la, la-la-la-la! Such a beautiful voice, no? Tell me, young Max, do you like this?'

'It's quite… different,' I manage and Hilda laughs.

'Yes, yes, it is so stunning. Oh, to be hearing it all for the first time again. So, tell me, you want your daddy to buy this for you? I will give you all these records too, so that you may learn all about good music, and your papa will pay me, what, one hundred rupees for the machine?'

I have a record player.

'This is some killing jungle music,' Flick exclaims, leafing his way disgustedly through the hefty stack of LPs that I have fallen heir to. 'I think that memsahib has been drinking to much ganga juice for her own good.'

'Murgia, Max,' Arnold echoes, 'you're never going to unload any of this stuff on anyone in this town who still has two ears left.'

'Oh, you never know,' I say quietly, having already sold an opera by Engelbert Humperdinck to one of the twins' entourage for twenty rupees, the lady in question being under the impression that she was buying the popular British crooner of the day; and Arthur has gladly parted with another twenty for a Chopin piano recital, so my teenage coffers are pretty near overflowing.

What, of course, I wasn't telling my friends was that I had been secretly quite enjoying playing my way through Mozart and particularly Wagner, and that I had already divided my pile of inherited Deutsche Grammophon recordings into 'sell' and 'don't sell' categories.

However, the sudden arrival of music into our previously quiet household hasn't all been a festival of culture, and when Alfie had informed me that there was a man at the bazaar who had a collection of 'English songs' for sale for only five rupees I had promptly handed over the cash, and our young bearer had returned staggering under the weight a pile of scratchy old seventy-eights.

Where these ancient relics had come from was anybody's guess, and they mainly consisted of thirties and forties American big bands like Benny Goodman and Glen Miller, but down at the bottom of the dusty pile of shellac lurked a treasure trove of nineteen-sixties pop, and Alfie and I had, with the aid of an *Archie* comic, been teaching ourselves to dance to 'Living Doll' and the unexpectedly rocky 'Move It'.

However, today is the day that my record player is going to be given something completely contemporary to play, and Mafzal drives all three of us down to the new market to hit the music shops and purchase something really hip.

There is, of course, no chance of my parents coughing up seventy rupees to purchase one of Mr Pang's under-the-counter Hong Kong imports, so my record buying power is going to be limited to what my forty rupees can purchase from the miscellany of dated singles available in the market, and, with my friends for back-up, we hit the town's biggest music seller and ask to see his English selection.

A small box of forty-fives is produced, and most of it is pretty dire stuff in the manner of Matt Monroe singing 'My Love is Like a Red, Red Rose', but, at the bottom of the pile, in a lurid acid-green vinyl pressing from the Gramophone Company of India, is 'All You Need is Love', 'Michelle' and – unbelievably – 'The Ballad of John and Yoko'.

The shopkeeper is asking for fifteen rupees a disc, but we collectively beat him down to forty for all three, and, short of going out and paying Arnold's dad seventy rupees for *Sergeant Pepper's Lonely Hearts Club Band*, as Flick has just done, I am now the proud owner of some of the trendiest pop in Chittagong.

Me and Mafzal, 1970

CHAPTER 16

ᎬᎡᎬᏟᏆᎾᎡ-ᏆᎾᎳᏁ

A fleet of young Irishmen is due to fly in later today to help install some brand-new plant that has been delivered to the mill from a foundry in Belfast, and the neighbouring jute wallahs have all chipped in to billet out the fleet of erectors, with everyone housing as many of the visiting Celts as they have room for.

Our bungalow has only one guest apartment, a large bedroom with a dressing room and en suite bath that sits separate from the house on the far edge of the front veranda, and thus we have been allocated Gerard, a trendy young Ulsterman with curly brown hair and sharp chin-level sideburns. Mafzal and I are sent to pick him up at the airport, and he strolls casually off the incoming flight from Singapore dressed in faded denims and an Abbey Road tee-shirt, carrying only a battered rucksack as his luggage, but to me he symbolises everything that a thirteen-year-old would want to aspire to be in nineteen sixty-nine.

'Hello, and you'll be Max, will you not?' he says in a strange accent that sounds like coarse Canadian mixed with sandpaper. 'And is this your driver? Pleased to meet you both!'

He shakes hands firmly with both of us and slaps me in the back, saying, 'And come on, is there a car or are we all walking home?' and, pulling ourselves together, we

lead him to the Vauxhall, where he flings his rucksack onto the floor and settles down on the back seat.

'Come away in and sit with me,' he drawls, ferreting in his bag. 'I've brought something for your mother, would she be liking cigarettes or perfume? Perfume, oh that's good, I can keep the fags for myself. And I got a tee-shirt for you, hope you like it!'

He flings something in a sealed plastic packet at me, and I turn it over to see the Yellow Submarine logo and realise that I have just been given a gift that Mr Pang could extort well over a hundred rupees for, not that I have any intention of selling it, and hugging the precious bounty to my chest I babble, 'It's fantastic. I don't know how to thank you, Gerard!'

'Away, and that's easy, now,' he grins. 'Just say "Thank you, Gerard". That ought to do it. Oh, and, Driver, you look to me like a smoking man, here's a pack of fags to you!'

We are his slaves.

There are jute wallahs living in the outback about three hours drive from Chittagong who are said to be existing on a diet of pure gin and boiled rice, but this doesn't make my dad any more comfortable with Gerard's custom of drinking a couple of bottles of beer after dinner each evening, and he practically transmogrifies into one of his old aunties when the chirpy Irishman offers a glass to me.

'Away now, Chic, let the boy have a taste,' he chides, seeing my father's look of white-faced disapproval. 'Max, have you any records that you could let me hear?'

'Just a couple of Beatles songs,' I mutter, my three trend-setting discs suddenly not so shiny any more. 'It's difficult to get LPs out here...'

'Well now, we'll make do with what we have then, won't we?' he says brightly, poking his head around the door of my room where his gifted tee-shirt sits – unopened – like a shrine. 'Oh my, now this is very smart, so it is. And "Michelle", that'll get you the girls for sure. Do you know any girls, Max?'

The object of all our desires is a young Slav called Lilliana, who is currently the uncontested queen of the swimming pool. She is, of course, quite unattainable, being fifteen years old with dark chestnut hair and flashing eyes, and she seems to exist perpetually in a tiny blue bikini that clings perilously to her small nut-brown body.

The lady in question is currently climbing out of the water in slow-motion, crystal beads of moisture flying form her hair and body as she stretches like a cat on the metal poolside ladder, while Arnold, Flick and myself sit glumly in the shallow end like three brass monkeys, completely invisible to this lithe bronze water goddess.

'Come on, boys,' Gerard's voice scolds as he walks by on the poolside above us, 'if you like the girl go and buy her a Coke or something. It's not like landing on the moon or anything!'

'Murgia,' Arnold sighs glumly, 'if only she didn't speak English, then I'd have an excuse for sitting here trembling with fear.'

'Don't worry, Fat Bugger,' Flick says laconically. 'She has no idea that you are even on the planet.'

'No, nor you also,' Arnold replies without rancour.

'Or any of us,' I say glumly as the object of our desires walks deliberately past the erectors' table and pauses long enough to let one of them invite her to sit down.

'I think we all need to learn how to make erections,' Arnold says in deadly seriousness.

three men in a boat

The huge reservoir at Kaptai in the Chittagong Hill Tracts is a popular weekend resort, and we have been here a few times on picnics with the mill under-managers and their families, but whereas the beautiful aquamarine waters of the lake are picturesque and inviting, the real fun of the place is getting on a speedboat and skimming across the water, taking your picnic to one of the many islands that dot the water's surface.

However, in our last September in the locality, a family that my parents know informs us that their company has a boat that is time-shared between managers, and, the following weekend being their turn, they invite us to join them on the water.

This information is relayed to me second-hand via my dad, and I look at him with breathless expectancy.

'Well?' I say anxiously. 'Don't keep me in suspense. Are we going or not?'

'Oh, you want to go, do you?' my dad teases. 'I told them you wouldn't be interested.'

'WHAT!?'

'I'm joking,' my dad laughs. 'Go and phone your idiot friends and OK it with their parents. We're going this Saturday.'

The lake cruiser, at first glance, looks disappointing, being a catamaran-style houseboat that looks a bit like a Portacabin on floats, but when we walk further along the pontoon jetty we see that a trim speedboat with a gleaming silver body bobs sedately behind it. The skipper, a wiry, bronze-skinned man with longish oiled hair and the obligatory pencil moustache, is standing on the dock with a cigarette in his hands, and he laughs softly at our saucer-like eyes.

'Yes, indeed, chotta sahibs,' he says in a very low voice, 'this very beautiful speedboat will, of course, be accompanying us on our journey, and I shall take you all water skiing from the island of my dear brother's widow, who will welcome you to her shore providing there is enough money on her farm to pay for the cattle feed...'

'We need to bribe the boatman?' I say to Flick in a loud whisper that my mother would have been proud of.

'This is Pakistan,' my friend replies drily. 'We need to bribe everyone. Achha, boat wallah, we will pay you five rupees for the cattle feed and the use of your sister-in-law's beach. Do we have agreement?'

The sky is a cloudless azure as the neat blue and white cruiser speeds across the large expanse of sapphire-green lake, and we all sit on deck with our feet trailing in the water and feeling the breeze in our hair as we fly along. The adults have wanted to go and visit the hydro-dam and power station before commencing our voyage, but our combined howl of disappointment was so heartfelt that the educational part of the trip has been foregone, and it has been decided to go out upon the water straight away.

The lake is a huge man-made reservoir created by the damming of the abundant Karnaphuli river into a lush natural valley, thus providing water and power for the city and its environs, and the flourishing green hills that surround us are said to be full of wild deer and even the occasional tiger.

It is a Saturday and there are lots of other pleasure craft on the water, and their foamy wakes rock the small hand-propelled sampans of local fishermen that meander across the lake, trying in vain to ply their trade amidst the influx of weekend holiday-makers.

However, as we get further away from the populated shore with its hotels and rest houses, small islands with the ghosts of submerged trees begin to appear as the boatman skilfully steers us through narrow channels of what have previously been low hills and forests. We maintain a good pace here at first, but eventually the boat begins to lose speed as more and more of these semi-submerged monoliths block our way, and we finally come to rest at a large island with a fine kutcha house made from bamboo and woven rush matting sitting about twenty feet above the high watermark.

As I'm nearest to the bow the skipper tosses me a rope, telling me to moor the boat to a stout tree-trunk that protrudes deformedly from the water, and I wade into the cool shallows while he goes up the house to converse with a raven-haired hill woman who has been eyeing us all suspiciously. There's a lot of conversation in a dialect that no one understands, but an agreement is finally reached and money changes hands, and our boatman waves us all onto the hot silver sands of the beach.

Now that we have paid our dues, small copper-skinned children with the slightly Nepalese eyes of the locality suddenly begin to appear from behind the dense trees at the rear of the house, and the boatman's sister-in-law herself, now wearing a friendly smile, brings down rush mats and a tea kettle for our use.

We boys all want to go swimming and water skiing straight away, but instead are assigned the task of setting up the picnic, and no one is allowed into the water until a fire has been lit and a marquee erected to shelter our party from the fierce afternoon sun.

The big boat has a small fridge which ensures a plentiful supply of cold drinks, and, with the kettle cheerfully boiling on the hob and boxes of sandwiches and cold salads stored carefully in the shade, we are finally let off the leash and onto the speedboat, and our friend the boatman lets out the throttle as we fly into to a clear channel and out across the water like a scudding rocket.

It is early September and, technically, well after the rainy season, but as we're all sitting on the beach, utterly exhausted, at around four o'clock, the boatman eyes some approaching clouds uneasily and says that the trip is over and that we must all return to the shore now.

Tents and food boxes are quickly packed on the houseboat and the speedboat is secured aft, as the skipper eyes the now blackening sky with apprehension, and we are all barely aboard before he casts off and speeds back down the treacherous channel with its acres of submerged forest.

Big drops of heavy rain are already making the previously calm water's surface boil, and a sudden wind picks up making the bulky craft pitch and toss as the master plots a homeward course along the now squally canal, trying to make it to open water before the might of the sudden storm hits us across the port bow.

The rain is torrential now and everyone is huddled in the tiny cabin and galley, trying to keep warm as great waves ravage the formerly glass-like water, but, as we crest yet another breaker with a communal groan, Flick whispers reassuringly into my ear, 'Do not be afraid. Allah would not permit us all to die when we are still virgins.'

Me aged twelve in Chittagong,
still just getting into my
Dundee school jumper

CHAPTER 18

the texas oil kings

The months fly past and a new luxury hotel opens in the city centre boasting a live band from Italy plus a private pool, and, on a hot night in our third sweltering summer, Flick takes me there on my fourteenth birthday to sample their new espresso bar.

'What's espresso, Flick?' I ask as his neat red Triumph cuts swiftly through the dark and misty night, 'and are we old enough to have it?'

'Who knows,' my friend replies philosophically. 'But we shall just go up to the counter and ask for it and see what we are handed.'

The bright lights of the tall white building ahead loom out of the haze to tell us that we're here, and, as Flick pulls up to a halt in front of the gleaming neon and chrome doorway, a smartly uniformed valet opens the doors for us and takes the Triumph off to a subterranean car park somewhere in the bowels of the huge hotel.

'What now?' I ask nervously, looking all about the cavernous white marble foyer, and Flick laughs.

'First, never show fear. Second, if we just keep walking we shall eventually arrive. There. We are here.'

A flashing red neon sign informs us that we have, indeed, found the espresso bar, and pretending that we

know what we're doing, we stride boldly into what a Karachi architect has visualised as a typical American diner and ask for a table.

'Is it just for two, Chotta Sahibs,' the sharply dressed bearer asks us in English, 'or will your respected parents also be joining you?'

'It is just as you see us, Burrah Bearer,' Flick replies looking surer of himself than he feels. 'We have come from our parents' homes to eat espresso at your fabled restaurant and, perhaps later, we shall go dancing.'

'Very good, Sahib,' the bearer says with only a very faint trace of a smile, 'then I shall personally take you to an excellent table and presently bring to you our menu of tonight.'

Turning deftly on the balls of his bare feet, he leads the way through his glittering eatery, which is practically deserted, and seats us at a chrome and glass table that overlooks the hotel's fairy-lit ultra-modern kidney-shaped pool.

'Chotta Sahibs, from today you will be my own special customers, and I hope that you shall return many times. This is to be your own table, and when you come again you must ask for Abdul, and I will escort you here myself, regardless of the hour of the day.'

'This is going to cost us a ten-rupee tip at the very minimum,' Flick whispers in my ear as we seat ourselves.

True to his word, Abdul quickly returns with tall die-cut menu cards that resemble New York skyscrapers, save for the Bengali script on their glossy front covers, and we both peer down a list of designer burgers and milk-shakes, our eyes unbelieving at the prices listed on the bill of fare.

'Ten rupees for a hamburger? Twenty for a cheeseburger?' I whisper. 'Have we got enough money with us or should we just run now while he's in the kitchen?'

'Keep your cool,' Flick replies sharply from behind his menu card. 'If we run now that fellow will see to it that we can never set foot in here again. I've got sixty bucks in my pocket, how about you?'

'About twenty and some change.'

'Very well, we will stay. Look out, he is coming. Don't order the cheapest thing on the menu or he will guess. We'll eat on my money and pay the tips with yours.'

Two burgers and two coffees later, we hand over a junior servant's monthly wage and tip our new friend Abdul an additional ten rupees.

'So, Chotta Sahibs, you will come again soon?' he preens, stroking his formidable moustache like a silent melodrama villain as he pockets my whole month's allowance.

'Most certainly, Abdul,' Flick agrees while I roll my eyes heavenwards out of the bearer's sightline, 'but tell me, it is very quiet here, is there no dancing tonight?'

'Oh no indeed, Sahib,' the bearer confirms, 'for today is Thursday and we have dancing only on Friday, Saturday and Sunday. See there, at the table by the counter, that is Antonio Sahib, the leader of our hand-picked orchestra from Italy. Tomorrow night he will be playing some very fine music indeed.'

We linger over our coffee while Antonio downs cup after cup of espresso, but eventually he says something vale-dictory to the door bearer and heads for the exit, and, seeing him go, Flick stands abruptly.

'Come on, he's going! Let's get the car. Tip the door bearer five rupees and keep your other five for the valet. Hurry up now, we don't have much time!'

We virtually fly down the lofty foyer and out into the misty night air, but the band leader is already vanishing into the heat haze, his glossy brilliantine a tiny star in the firmament when the Herald is eventually brought up from below.

'Go!' Flick commands and pit-stops off before I can even get my door closed.

'What are we doing, Flick?' I demand as we career after the Italian's retreating figure.

'Making friends and saving money,' my friend grins, winding down his window. 'Signor Antonio, may we offer you a lift?'

Flick motions me into the cramped back seat to make way for our guest, and the grateful musician clambers into my place at the front of the dark vehicle.

'This is very kind of you,' he smiles, all teeth, like a shark. 'This humidity does nothing for my rheumatics, and although we are resident here they have given us quarters at the Hotel Shajahan. That is on your way, no?'

'Certainly,' Flick lies, and I hope he actually knows where the hostelry in question is located, 'we shall be pleased to drop you there, won't we, Max?'

'Oh, I'm sure we will,' I say sarcastically, but my dry wit is wasted on my companions, who are already deep in conversation about music in Karachi nightclubs, and I settle down to watch the coloured lights and bright neons of the town as Flick drives us deftly through the crowded streets. A large teapot perpetually fills row after row of cups with Lipton tea, while a bespectacled dentist grins the praises of Colgate, and it's as though I am back in Britain again, save for the scores of bullock carts and rickshaws that curse their way along the freshly hosed-down boulevards, red tail-lights reflecting like blood trails on the wet tarmac.

A sign in glowing purple and gold letters above a faded but grand archway announces that we have arrived at Antonio's place of residence, and Flick's car navigates a small parade of shops to the front door.

'Ciao, and thank you so much, gents,' he smiles, peering short-sightedly into the dark interior of the car, 'Please to accept these tickets for tomorrow night with my compliments, and tell them to put you at my table. We start playing at nine, so get there before if your work permits. What did you say you do?'

My throat closes up trying to make up some lie, but quick as a flash Flick replies, 'Oh, we are in the oil business.'

CHAPTER 19

and it's goodnight from him

Our planned night of revelry on the hotel's dance floor is quickly quashed when my parents discover the nature of our proposed expedition, and even Flick's more tolerant guardians balk at the idea when they learn that alcohol is going to be freely served. Undeterred we put our free passes up for sale on the black market to recoup our night's expenditure, Flick's elder brother being the highest bidder, and he reports back that the myopic Antonio is completely unaware that his gifted tickets have been switched on him.

'Never fear,' Flick consoles me as we sit disconsolate by the poolside at the club the next morning, 'for we shall both attend the dancing when we are eighteen and irresistible to women.'

We both laugh heartily at the unimaginable notion of being either eighteen or irresistible, and proceed to sit for hours sheltering from the baking sun, planning our fantasy grand cotillion when no one can prevent us sweeping some mythical members of the opposite sex out onto the sea of coloured lights that is the new hotel's dance floor.

'It will indeed be a grand day, my friend,' Flick says laconically. 'Let us hope that you will be still here to celebrate it with me.'

I stare dumbly at Flick, my mouth open like a goldfish.

'Why shouldn't I be here?' I ask, and my friend just looks at me pityingly.

'The rains will be here soon and that will be your third monsoon in our country,' he says gently. 'After that your pop's contract will be up for renewal...'

His unexpected words have a chilling resonance to them, and I realise with a jolt that my days here may, indeed, be numbered. For, unlike the good old days of my early childhood in India when the British were incumbent for the long haul, we modern-day burrah sahibs live very much on borrowed time, and the Chittagong expat community all measure their existence strictly within the confines of the family breadwinner's contracted terms.

'Oh well,' I think, 'what will be will be, and anyway, the rains aren't even here yet,' but even as we speak a cloud passes over the glaring white sun and the first tentative drops of the coming monsoon start splattering like scalding fat on the baking poolside paving slabs. Laughing, everyone makes a dash for the cover of the big coloured umbrellas, a sigh of gleeful reprieve echoing around the assembled populace now that the weather has finally broken, but for the first time in my young life the coming of the rains does not bring me the customary feeling of relief.

When I had first arrived here three years earlier, a bewildered little boy in short pants struggling valiantly to remember my basic Urdu vocabulary, it had seemed that I had all the time in the world to explore this wonderful country, but our allocated three monsoons have already fallen in speedy succession and it is rapidly dawning on me that I am now almost six feet tall and that it might be time to leave.

However, I am still floundering within the marshy territory of my own naivety, and I tell myself that the end of Dad's contract will merely mean a short few months in Scotland followed by another three summers in the east; and I duly become very excited at the prospect of going home on leave. My previous life there now conveniently forgotten, Dundee's presbyterian grey architecture quickly metamorphoses into the hip Riverdale of *Archie* comics in my teenage mind, and I suddenly visualise the myriad of records that will hang like plump cherries from the laden boughs of abundant British music stores, and mentally fill carrier bags full of contraband goodies to bring back for Flick and Arnold.

'I'd never thought of going on home leave, Flick,' I say enthusiastically. 'Just think of all the great stuff I can bring back for you from Britain,' but my friend just looks at his feet and shakes his head sadly.

'Bhai, you may not come back,' he says quietly, and, for the second time that day, the bottom falls out of my world.

It has, of course, never entered my head that with the ever-worsening political situation my father will not negotiate a second contract, although the continuous presence of lorries full of heavily armed West Pakistani soldiers in the streets should have been a clue that all is far from right in Wonderland. But I am fourteen and living life to the full, easily dovetailing my copious school work with flying through the hot nights in Flick's neat red Triumph or swimming in the cool greeny-blue waters of the lake, and there is no reason in my mind why any of this should ever stop.

Yet stop it does, and my dad, reading the writing on the wall with incredible accuracy, declines a second term at his beloved mill and my family starts on the agonising business of settling up our affairs and selling off the surprising number of possessions that we have accrued in our three years in the town; and, just as the vicar had foretold all those years ago when we had first arrived, there is a queue right down the hill at the church Saturday sale waiting to pick over our departing remains.

I sell a long-disused Tri-ang railway and a Scalextric set that reach over two hundred rupees each on the open market, and my family will eventually leave the town with over three thousand rupees in non-convertible notes that we will trade for black-market American dollars with some shady soldiers in the middle of the night at Karachi airport.

I spend our last scant months in severe denial, however, existing in a sort of limbo world of my own making, concentrating only on the immediate tasks to be performed, and deliberately allocating no time to visualising what my future in a Scottish comprehensive might hold. The rains finally cease, and our last fortnight turns into an endless round of farewell parties and formal receptions that, blissfully, leave me little time to think, and, as the days fly by, I still point-blank refuse to believe that all of this is soon to be nothing more than a memory of a three-year period of contentment.

Everyone is coming to the airport to see us off so there have been no good-byes as yet, and it is literally not until I am standing in our suddenly bereft lounge, all our knick-knacks either packed away or sold and the bare walls looking as they had on that fateful first day, that I finally accept that we will never be returning to this happy place again. The servants have lined up to bid us farewell like something out of a house-party period drama, and the cook stands philosophically by the door of his pantry, ready to adopt whoever will follow in our footsteps. He meets my eyes and gives me his smiling blessing as we walk out to the waiting car, but Alfie unexpectedly breaks ranks and hugs me violently, bursting into tears, and I cling to him desperately, suddenly unwilling to leave my beloved home and my good friend.

'Come on, come on, we've a plane to catch,' my dad scolds from the car with feigned gruffness, and I say a hasty last goodbye to the tearful bearer and dash quickly into the waiting Vauxhall.

'So, our three stolen years are finally over,' my dad says over my shoulder with put-on cheerfulness, as I crane my neck trying to catch a last glimpse of Chittagong and all our waving friends from the tiny porthole window of the old Fokker Friendship, 'and we're going home.'

I don't answer straight away, and, turning my face to the window so that he can't see the traitorous tears that are trickling down my cheeks, I finally reply, 'But this is our home, isn't it? Why can't we just stay here, Dad?'

'No, Chummo,' Dad says softly, using my long-neglected pet name, 'we're only guests here and I'm afraid that we've already outstayed our welcome. We need to go back to our own nest now.'

'Yes, I suppose we do,' I sigh, as the plane swoops over the blue waters of the Bay of Bengal, and I breathe in deeply, as if summoning up the strength to face the next chapter of my life, a new adventure that would soon commence in a crowded cinema in Hamburg on a hot August night...

Our house, Chittagong

glossary

Achha: Yes, OK

Anglo-Indian: An Indian or Pakistani who follows the Christian faith and dresses in western clothes. Can also be used as an insult meaning 'mulatto' or 'half-breed'.

Armoire: Wardrobe.

Awami League: At the time of this book, the political party speaking out for the rights of East Pakistan.

Ayah: Nanny.

Baboo: An office clerk.

Baksheesh: Tips, alms, freebies.

Bearer: A general domestic servant, a cross between a footman and a valet in a house, or a waiter in a restaurant or club. A 'Burrah Bearer' would be butler or head waiter.

Bhai: Brother

Bhakti Fish: Particularly delicious fish native to Bengal.

Bioscope: A cinema, a film show, or just a motion picture.

Blighty or Belite: Great Britain or British.

Botchi: Cook.

Buckas Wallah: A travelling pedlar who carries his saleable goods in a tin box. If used as an insult, inferring that someone is a crook of no fixed abode.

Burrah Bearer: A butler or head waiter.

Burrah Maidan: Usually, the main lawn or park of an estate or mill, but can also refer to a football field or cricket pitch.

Burrah Mali: Head gardener.

Burrah Sahib: Boss or Sir.

Chalo: Get a move on!

Cheena Bedamm: Mixture of fried spicy nuts and pulses. Usually known as Bombay Mix outside of India.

Chorr Wallah: Thief.

Chotta Sahib: Young Master.

Clootie Dumpling: A Scottish Christmas pudding, boiled in a cloth or 'cloot' for several hours.

Diniyat: Religious instruction for Muslims.

Durwan: Guard or security man.

Englishman: In the Indian sub-continent, anybody white.

Erectors: British people sent, normally from Belfast, to install machinery and heavy plant.

Dhobi: Man who does your washing, usually by bashing it with a stone or stick. Murderous on buttons.

Ganga Juice: This can refer to many intoxicating substances, in Flick's case, however, he means a liquor that is distilled from coconut sap.

Gundas: Oiks, rabble, peasants.

Hai Rabba: Oh My God!

Hartal: General strike. Usually, roads are barricaded and everything is brought to a halt, and anyone found breaking the mob-imposed curfew is liable to be beaten or, in very rare cases, killed.

Jaao!: Scoot, scram, buzz off!

Jute Godowns: Jute warehouses.

Jute Wallahs: Those who work in the jute industry.

Kutcha Houses: Kutcha means 'raw' in Hindi/Urdu, and a kutcha house is a dwelling made of non-permanent materials, normally bamboo and rush matting.

Lunghi: A knee-length strip of fabric worn around the waist like a kilt by men. (Totally the only way to dress in very hot weather!)

Mah-jong: A Chinese game, the same idea as card games such as whist, but played using ivory tiles. There are four players to a set, and each player usually has a wooden 'wall' to keep their tiles concealed from other players. Highly addictive to those who love cards or board games.

Mali: Gardener.

Memsahib: Madam.

Moonya Bird: Small song bird.

Muhammad Ali Jinnah: The founder of Pakistan. This quiet lawyer with his signature fur cap has been historically eclipsed by the showier Gandhi, but was a statesman of exceptional ability and only lacks a bio-pic by Dicky Attenborough to put him onto the same celebrity status as his Indian counterpart.

Murgia!: The favourite expression of my good friend, Arnold Pang. Murgia literally means 'death' or 'dead', but in Arnold's case he really means, 'I'm dead'.

Paan: Betelnut leaf. A juicy green leaf that is spread with spices and rolled into a cone and then chewed, giving off a red liquid that led many Victorian Englishmen in India to believe that the natives were all TB sufferers, as they appeared to always be spitting blood. Enjoyed by low caste workers and grand Indian ladies alike.

Pataka: A firecracker, usually ignited by lighting the blue touch-paper, but sometimes being a tightly wrapped ball of gunpowder and small stones bound in coloured tissue paper and thrown hard at walls or the ground to explode.

Peon: A messenger or low worker in an office, or, generally, one of low caste.

Piaju-Wallah: A man who makes and sells onion bhaji on the street.

Pish-Pash, *Glacé Beef* and *Potato Chops*: Staple British-Indian food. Pish-Pash is chicken and rice stewed together in milk and broth, often a nursery or sickroom dish; Glacé Beef is beef pounded into tenderness and then served in a thick cornflour gravy; and Potato Chops are minced beef wrapped in mashed potato and then rolled in breadcrumbs and fried.

Prickly-heat: Particularly nasty heat rash.

Puja: A Hindu religious holiday or festival.

Purdah Women: Muslim women who keep their faces covered.

Pye Dog or *Pariah Dog*: A breed of Mongrel dog unique to the Indo-Pakistan sub-continent.

Rasgullâs: Sickly-sweet Indian sweetmeat. Highly addictive.

Shakespeare Wallahs: You've see the movie. Troops of, usually British, actors who perform Shakespeare's plays in Indian/Pakistani schools.

Shippy Fellows: Chinese merchant sailors.

Singara: A fried pastry shell stuffed with spicy vegetables. Similar to a samosa but with softer pastry. Addictive.

Tamasha: A fête, function or gala.

Topis: Those funny domed hats you see white people wearing in old movies about India.

Victrola: A wind-up gramophone

Zinzabad!: For ever!